Praise for *Paid*

"I have been working on my book for the last nine years. This system helped me work through my fear and anxiety. I wrote and finished my book in a few weeks."- Casheena Parker, author of *No Longer Broken: Heal from Your Trauma and Empower Your Future*

"What I loved about this information is that we were provided with the proper tools and guidance to self-publish a book correctly."- Ja'Net Dessesseau author of *Just Gracefully Driven: Regaining Clarity on Your Purpose, Dreams, and Goals*

"I have been saying I wanted to write my book for so long. I would start and stop, and then I just felt like it would never happen. I love the support and felt like this information was the answer to my prayers. I was able to accomplish my goal of writing and finishing my book in just a few weeks."- Saundra Golden, author of *Make It Stop! A Young Woman's Guide to Overcome or Prevent Dating Abuse*

Published
and Paid

Published and Paid

Write, Self-Publish, and Launch Your Non-Fiction Book in 90 Days or Less

Jasmine Womack

Jasmine Womack. © 2021

All rights reserved. No part of this book may be reproduced, stored, or transmitted by any means- whether auditory, graphic, mechanical, or electronic- without written permission of both publisher and author, except in the case of brief excerpts used in critical articles and certain other noncommercial uses permitted by copyright law. Unauthorized reproduction of any part of this work is illegal and punishable by law.

ISBN-13: 978-0-9906099-5-7 - Paperback
eISBN: 978-0-9906099-6-4 - eBook

Printed in the United States of America   0 5 2 4 2 1

∞This paper meets the requirements of ANSI/NISO Z39.48-1992 (Permanence of Paper)

Cover Design: Jamal Smith of MalMedia
Photo: Mecca Gamble of Mecca Gamble Photography
Editors: Ethleen Sawyerr of Speak Write Play and Dr. Joel Boyce of JCB Educational Services

For more information, please visit:
www.publishedandpaidbook.com
www.jasminewomack.com

What Type of Book Should You Write to Boost Your Brand or Career?

Take the quiz at www.startmybookquiz.com!

This book is for the author hiding inside of you.
Your life...your expertise...is a story worth writing.

And someone is waiting for you to share it.

Contents

Introduction   xi

Chapter 1
The Mindset of a Best-Selling Author   1

Chapter 2
Niche Your Topic   13

Chapter 3
Embrace Your Voice & Share Your Story   29

Chapter 4
Organizing Your Content   39

Chapter 5
Writing Your Book   43

Chapter 6
Creating Your Money Title   49

Chapter 7
Designing Your Book Cover   55

Chapter 8
The Revision Process   59

Chapter 9
Marketing, Promotions, and Sales   71

Chapter 10
Your Next Steps   99

Epilogue   105

Introduction

Welcome to *Published and Paid: Write, Self-Publish, and Launch Your Book in 90 Days or Less,* and thank you for purchasing this book. My hope is that by the time you reach the end of this book, you will have the tools and knowledge to write, self-publish, and launch your book successfully.

If you are reading this book, then I know that you have a story you want to share. However, you have been struggling to get your ideas on paper and move forward to share your message with the world.

You've been overwhelmed and overthinking. Trust me, I know how it feels to start, stop, start, stop, and start again. This was my experience for ten years with writing my first book. You edit as you go and try to make your book the perfect piece of writing as you draft it. Doubts and uncertainty fill your mind, and your excitement turns to excuses when you realize that your ideas don't come out as easily as you'd like.

You may feel a bit unqualified. You may not have a large brand or a ton of followers. You may even find yourself thinking, *Will anyone actually read my book? What will people think? What will my family say?*

Or maybe, you're just plain stuck. You've hit the writer's block wall and are sitting there. You have no clue how to get off, and you know that you need some help to finish your book.

I wrote this book to remind you that you CAN write and publish your book with ease in just a few weeks. Even if you don't have fancy titles or credentials, you can do it. And even if you've been struggling for years, it can be done.

Some call me the "Six-Figure Storyteller." Others say I'm the "Harriet Tubman of Self-Publishing." I've been a writing consultant and educator for over 12 years, but I've been in the online space since 2016. Since then, I've helped over 1,000 authors successfully write, self publish, and use their books to build profitable, impactful platforms.

I am the author of five books and have helped over 1,000 authors bring their stories to life, but it wasn't always this way.

I remember when I was in college, and a close friend and his associates were writing chapbooks, which are mini-books with a cardstock cover that were stapled together at the seam. The books were flimsy, but even with the cheaply produced books, they were accomplishing a lot more than others our age. I was inspired. I'd always been a great writer, but they had more courage than me at the time to publish their books. Deep down, I knew if they could do it, I could do it, too.

I never wrote my book in college even though my friends did. I said I'd do it the next year...and the next year...and the next year. One year turned into five years. Before I knew it, ten years had passed. Ten years of incomplete Word documents and papers balled up and tossed in the trash can. Ten years of hope deferred and a dream unrealized. Ten years of saying I was going to do something that I never did.

My dream remained unfulfilled until the time finally came. I had been holding the goal in my heart and knew that if I didn't make a move, it would never materialize. During this time, I was pregnant with my second child and was placed on bed rest to prevent premature labor. There I was, day in and day out, with the walls and TV staring at me. I knew that God had given me this time to finish what I started long ago, so I made the decision to make good use of my time and go for it.

With a simple shift of my thinking, ten years of struggle turned into a complete book within two weeks. I later wrote my second book in 24 hours.

Writing and self-publishing my book changed my life. I've had the opportunity to work with celebrities and CEOs of multi-million dollar companies. I've been featured in major publications such as Forbes and HuffPost. I was also able to leave my job, become a full time entrepreneur, build a 7-figure business and help other career professionals use their books to accomplish their career and financial goals. None of this would have been possible if I had not written and published my book.

The purpose of *Published and Paid: Write, Self-Publish, and Launch Your Book in 90 Days or Less* is to explain the writing process step by step and provide you with the necessary direction so you can bring your goal of becoming an author to life.

I've taken the strategies that I teach my writing clients and put them into this book. The content in this book won't work on its own. This will only work if you read each page and chapter, and implement what you learn. If you skip chapters, stop reading, or decide to put it off, then your book will remain a distant dream. Therefore, I want you to take these strategies to heart and put them into immediate action.

Stop wondering, stop waiting, and stop working to write the perfect book. The perfect book is the book that comes from your heart. Once you read *Published and Paid: Write, Self-Publish, and Launch Your Book in 90 Days or Less*, you will be equipped to move forward and share your story with the world. You don't have to wait for a better time to do this.

The best time is now.

Peace, Love, and E.M.P.A.C.T.,

Jasmine

Chapter 1

The Mindset of a Best-Selling Author

What is a mindset and what does mindset have to do with being an author?

The term, "mindset," refers to established beliefs or attitudes you have about yourself and your ability to accomplish things and deal with situations that arise throughout your life.

I know that "mindset" is a term that's thrown around loosely and is often overused, but a growth mindset is extremely important for you to develop. Your mindset is the element that will determine your success or failure. You can have all the strategy and know-how in the world. If your mindset doesn't align with your goals, you will not accomplish what you set out to attain—plain and simple.

Start by assessing and identifying the current state of your mindset, so you can continue to grow and develop into the best person, leader, author, and entrepreneur you can be.

Before you do this, remember that you have the power to change your thinking.

You must know that you are greater than your current reality. You are greater than your current attitudes and beliefs. Your attitudes and beliefs often come from your childhood, are rooted in core experiences you had growing up, or have been adopted throughout adulthood. These attitudes and beliefs are the products of circumstances that changed who you are or what your perspective on life is.

Some of your established attitudes and beliefs also can be traced back to things that people may have said to you or even spoken over you during a period of time in your life. Regardless of whether or not their words were true, you began to believe what they said. You internalized their words and shrunk back, or allowed their words to take root and turn you into a different person. I want you to know right now that you have power over all of it. You have power and control over the attitudes and beliefs that have been established in your mind. You have the power to change them, and you have the authority to change your thinking. You have the ability to change yourself.

When it comes to mindsets, there are generally two types: a growth mindset and a fixed mindset. Let's look at both of these.

Someone who has a growth mindset believes that things, people, and even themselves will develop with persistence and perseverance. If you have a growth mindset, you believe that you will get through obstacles if you keep going. You'll make it to the other side. Once you do, there's a better opportunity for you. If you have a growth mindset, you tend to focus on the *process* instead of just on the *outcome*. You find the blessing in the journey, not just in reaching the destination. This means that you embrace everything that comes along with the process, including the challenges and obstacles you may encounter as part of the adventure.

If you have a growth mindset, you also tend to view failure as an opportunity for reflection, evaluation, and growth. I want you to look at the characteristics of a growth mindset and determine whether or not you embody them in your thinking.

Now, those with a fixed mindset tend to focus only on the *outcome*. Someone with a fixed mindset often avoids challenges. This means that you begin to avoid something the moment it starts looking or feeling a bit more difficult than you want it to be. You don't want to confront the conflict.

For example, Jasmyne was a client of mine who set out to start writing her book. While she was in the process of writing her book, she also transitioned from her job into full-time entrepreneurship, planned a wedding, and was in the process of closing on a home.

Someone with a fixed mindset would have looked at this entire circumstance and identified plenty of excuses not to write or finish their book. They would have put it off until later, citing a lack of time and ability to focus.

However, I didn't even find out that Jasmyne had all of this transition going on until her book was being printed. She didn't look for excuses. She embraced the challenges, gave it her all, and came out winning in the end. Jasmyne had a growth mindset.

If you find that you have a fixed mindset, you might be

wondering how you can transform your thinking and develop more of a growth mindset. Your ability to grow and change depends on the amount of work you are willing to do.

It's not enough to financially invest in courses, purchase books, or attend conferences. You also have to make the investment in yourself, which is where you actually apply what you learn and put it to work in your life.

For example, simply purchasing a book isn't enough; you also must take your time to read it and apply what you read. By implementing the strategies in your life and perhaps taking it a step further by purchasing an accompanying workbook or course to dig deeper into those concepts, you can begin to learn, grow, and develop.

Doing the work also means that you are willing to learn about yourself and be honest with yourself—about yourself. It means that you stop pointing the finger at other people and different circumstances. Instead, start looking at yourself to determine how you can respond differently when you are faced with a challenging situation.

Even in the worst situations, people with a growth mindset will not blame anyone else. They'll self assess, process, and think, *You know what? I understand that this traumatic incident occurred, and I didn't have control over it. What can I control? I can control how I move forward. I can control my choices. I can control how I approach each and every day. I can control the level at which I forgive. I can control what I'm willing to let go. I can control my level of optimism.*

You have the power to make life what you desire. There

are huge benefits to having a growth mindset because once you develop this flexible, creative-centered mentality, you will begin to understand that you have the power to shape your future through *your* focus, *your* hard work, and *your* maximum effort.

You will begin to assess yourself instead of criticizing yourself. You will begin to seek ways to improve yourself. Therefore, when you encounter challenges, face failures, or perform worse than you expected or less than you desired, you will give yourself grace instead of being hard on yourself. Use every situation as a learning point to grow and develop. Learn about yourself and discover how you can improve for the next time.

As an author, you must embrace leadership and work to build a thought-leadership platform. There are going to be people who will not only read your book, but also they're going to listen to everything you say. You will develop and gain one of the most powerful forces in this world: the force of influence. You will have the power and ability to impact the decisions someone else makes. And you will have the power and opportunity to influence how someone else thinks and feels.

Your words will plant seeds of change in the hearts, minds, and emotions of others, and those seeds have the ability to influence their actions.

That's responsibility.

That is influence.

As an author, it's critical that you develop a growth mindset because in order to teach and lead others to growth, you must be willing to grow yourself. You cannot help others do what you are unwilling to do, so this is where integrity matters. With the power of influence, you can do more harm than good if you're leading for the wrong reasons or leading from a toxic space. Therefore, I encourage you to pay attention to your thinking.

A very easy way to assess your thinking is to stop complaining.

You will find 30 Days to Not Complaining in your resources kit. Visit www.myppbook.com to access this free resource.

In this challenge, you cannot complain about anything—not the weather, your children, your spouse, your aches, your pains, or your food—for 30 days. When you find yourself complaining about something, stop immediately. Instead, verbally make a statement of gratitude about the thing that you were complaining about. This simple exercise will help you radically shift your thinking, reshape your thoughts and move from a fixed mindset of complaining and pessimism to a mindset of growth and gratitude.

This will help you reshape your thoughts and move from a fixed mindset of complaining and pessimism to a mindset of growth and gratitude.

By steering your thoughts toward gratitude for what you have, you will begin to change the way you feel and think about everything around you.

Why Does Your Mindset Matter?

Why are we talking about your mindset in a book designed to help you write your book? Well, it's because your thoughts shape your life. Your thoughts impact what you do, how you feel, and the way you think. There are going to be points and times throughout your writing journey when negative thoughts will enter your mind. Doubt and a lack of confidence may attempt to bring a stop to your journey. When this happens, you must operate from a growth mindset to embrace the process, so you can move past those moments of blockage to accomplish your goal.

Let's be totally honest. You're not going to just close your eyes and have your book fall into your lap completely finished. There's work that you will be required to do during the process. As we know, things happen. Life happens, and societal issues occur. There will be moments of happiness and accomplishment, and there will also be moments of frustration; you must be able to push past them.

With a growth mindset, the ability to push past the difficult moments is rooted in your thoughts because your thoughts frame your concept and view of yourself including what you believe you are capable of accomplishing. Therefore, your mindset impacts your results!

Your words, responses, and opinions affect everything you do. They also help to frame the worldview of your children and establish the attitudes and beliefs to which they are going to revert when they get older.

How to Develop and Cultivate a Growth Mindset

There are three steps to developing your mindset and thinking:

- Step One: Plan and identify
- Step Two: Take action
- Step Three: Evaluate and engage

Let's break it down.

Step 1: Plan and identify
Let's take a closer look.

In step one, you're going to identify your current state, where you are, what you're dealing with, what you've dealt with in the past, and how you handled it.

Generally, we all have patterns. You have a pattern in the way in which you handle conflict and confrontation. You have a way in which you address and deal with challenges when they arise. Start by identifying where you are now and what you've done in the past that has contributed to your current circumstances. Also, identify your strengths and potential areas of growth. To do this, I want you to reflect on three situations that you faced in the last 30 to 90 days. Consider how you handled them. Identify the patterns regarding your approach to situations when they arise in your life.

Step 2: Take action
Next, you must take action. When you take action, move forward to analyze what you need to do in order to

get a better result the next time. Process the steps you need to take so you can improve your response and your overall situation. Even if you responded well, how can you capitalize on that and do even better?

In this step, you'll also monitor your self-talk. How do you tend to talk to yourself? Do you often curse people out in your head? That's self-talk. Do you tend to pray or say different motivational and uplifting things to yourself? That's self-talk, too. Positive self talk cannot be limited to reciting affirmations when you're looking in the bathroom mirror. Positive self talk is also needed when someone cuts you off on the highway and you fume at the ears, cursing them out in your head.

I want you to check your self-talk. How do you talk to yourself every single day? What do you say about yourself? What do you say about other people? When you look in the mirror, do you say, "Oh man, I'm so fat. I've gained so much weight," or do you say, "You know what... God, thank you for giving me this body. Thank you for giving me another opportunity to create the body that I want".

Immediately after, my feelings and my focus changed.

In this same way, you must monitor your self talk about your writing and your potential for success, or else you will end up talking yourself down and focusing on your limitations instead of talking yourself up and bringing the possibilities into existence.

Each perspective represents opposite ends of the reaction spectrum. Which end are you on?

Self-talk was something that I personally had to make sure I paid attention to after I had my second child by C-section.

My stomach wasn't "snatched" like it was pre-pregnancy. I would look in the mirror every single day and put myself down.

Then I realized what I was doing and said to myself, "You know, Jas, you're going to continue to manifest the things you speak. You must change the way you feel and change your words."

I then began to speak positively over myself and express gratitude for my body.

You have to monitor your self-talk 24/7. Be intentional and turn your negative words around into something positive.

As you monitor your self-talk, I also want you to set improvement goals. When was the last time you set personal development goals for yourself? This goes beyond reading a book once or twice a month. It's when you take your goals a step further.

An example of a personal development goal is to compliment yourself and someone else each day. Compliment yourself and acknowledge your accomplishments because you know that you bring value into the world.

I want you to create time parameters for these goals. I want you really to think about it and then set a goal that is achievable and growth-oriented.

For example, one way to create a growth-oriented goal is to commit to complimenting yourself and someone else each day for 30 days.

Step 3: Evaluate and engage

Now, step three is the part that many people miss. They

do not self assess or thoughtfully conduct a thorough self-reflection.

Set a day or time to conduct thoughtful self-reflection and analysis. This can be done at the end of every day or every week.

Journaling is a tool that is immensely useful for this. This is when you privately write down and share events that happened in your day such as what went well or what didn't go as well as you'd hoped.

When journaling, you can respond to the following questions:

- Were you faced with any difficult circumstances, or were you challenged by something or someone? If so, how did you respond?
- How did you feel?
- How did you talk about the situation?
- What did you do well in the situation?
- What could you improve? How could you do even better next time?

Too often, we don't stop to do real self-reflection and evaluation to determine the gaps that exist in the midst of responses, thoughts, and feelings toward situations throughout the day.

It's so important to reflect on how you can address things moving forward and really make a mental note of what to pay attention to. When you incorporate this practice into your life, over time, you will find that when challenges and negative situations arise, you will address them in a totally different way.

For example, these difficult situations could include an argument with your sibling, or even your spouse. Reflect on your role in the situation. Instead of pointing the finger at the other person, take time to identify your part in what happened. What went well? What didn't go so well? How can you improve your response and feelings moving forward to get a better result?

The truth of the matter is that whatever you have going on in your personal life is going to carry over into your approach when writing your book, and it's definitely going to carry over into your attitude while building your business. It will also affect how you relate and interact with your clients and customers because you cannot separate your personal life and business activity.

You may be able to compartmentalize your emotions and personal circumstances for a short period of time, but it will only be a matter of time before the cracks appear. You will always revert back to the level of your training. Whatever is in you eventually will come out, so it's extremely important that you make an intentional effort to do the work on your inner self. When you encounter difficult customers or tiring clients, when you face challenges in your business, or even when you go to speak and you may not feel your best, you will be prepared to operate from a growth mindset of progression instead of a fixed mindset of limitation and pessimism.

Chapter 2

Niche Your Topic

Before you write your book, identify your niche topic and audience as well as plan the goals you desire to reach beyond your book being published.

I want you to be able to transition your mindset from a general approach and desire of writing your book to target a very specific audience and industry. This simple shift is going to set you up for maximum success beyond the book. Therefore, after your book is released, you'll be prepared to create information-based products, services, product suites, speeches, and more. You'll know exactly what to do, what to provide, and who will benefit most from what you have to offer.

For example, say that you desire to write a book about abuse. "Abuse" is very broad, so you will need to niche your topic down. First, consider what type of abuse you'll be writing about. Many different types of abuse exist: domestic violence, financial abuse, emotional abuse, childhood abuse, or mental abuse, etc.

If you want to write a book to empower women, you will have to narrow your topic even more because "women's empowerment" is extremely broad. I want to challenge you to focus on a specific area of women's empowerment. Will your book concentrate on confidence building, entrepreneurship, women's empowerment through economic and personal growth, women's empowerment through emotional wellness, or women's empowerment through learning how to obtain more work-life balance? These distinctions and specificities are important.

If you're a consultant and you desire to write a book for other consultants, what will your aim and focus be? Who is your specific audience? Are you going to write a book for educational consultants, leadership consultants, diversity and inclusion consultants, or consultants who focus on developing a remote workforce?

It's extremely important to narrow down and focus on the industry and audience to whom you are going to speak. Who will the information in your book target? To what audience is the majority of your information directed? If you were to sit down to have lunch and mentor someone as he or she asked you questions, who would this person be? What industry would they be in? Why would he or she need your help? What challenges would he or she have? If you're able to answer these questions, I guarantee that you will increase your clarity, organization, and progress. Your content will become even easier to write because you'll know exactly who you're addressing and why you are writing to them.

As another example, let's say you are a life coach or that you want to write a book for life coaches. Are you writing a life coaching book for women or business owners? Is it for corporate executives or single parents? Is it for teen mothers? Is it for people with chronic illnesses? Is it for people who've been ostracized by their families, or for those who are trying to find their space and sense of belonging in the world? Life coaching, in particular, is broad, so you must narrow down to focus on the type of life coaching you actually will discuss. Your book about life coaching cannot be broad, and it cannot be for "everyone".

I've worked with many clients who wanted to write books about mental health, but we had to clarify their niche because mental health is such a broad field. For example, they had to select their niche within mental health in regard to mood, anxiety, depression, eating disorders, trauma, or substance abuse. You also can break down mental health even further into other subtopics such as: mental health for single mothers, mental health for working mothers who are also entrepreneurs, mental health for supervisors, executives, and those in high pressure jobs, mental health for leaders, mental health for pastors, etc. The more specific your audience is, the more accurately you will reach your readers. This will matter as you write your book because niching your topic is a critical element to writing and publishing a results-focused book.

Most importantly, you must resist the temptation to believe your book can apply to everyone. Avoid the belief that your book can be about mental health in general. You must narrow your subject all the way down because, while there may be different audiences that might benefit from your book, you don't want to market or speak to the outliers or to everyone. For example, if you write a book about mental health for single mothers, there are likely still going to be some married women who can benefit from it. Regardless, the book primarily will target single mothers who are handling work, child rearing, finances, and even their own minds and sanity, and your content must speak to this. If you write to everyone, you write to no one, so you must be as specific as possible when selecting your ideal audience and niche topic.

Ask yourself these questions:

- Who is my target audience?
- Is it men or women?
- What *kind* of men/women comprise my audience?
- What are their psychographics (how do they think)?
- What do they like?
- What type of clothes do they wear?
- What type of shoes do they wear?
- What type of car do they drive?
- Where do they shop?
- Do they prefer Walmart or Target?
- Do they prefer Marshall's or Saks Fifth Avenue?
- How old are they?
- How much money do they make? What is their level of education?
- What is their marital status?
- Do they have children?
- How do they raise their children?
- Do they send their children to public school, private school, or homeschool them? Why?

You must know very clearly who you're targeting.

Remember, your product and service are the solution to someone else's problem, and you need to be able to articulate that and show them how. You can't do that if you don't know or understand the challenges and mindset of your readers. If you're trying to figure out what their challenge is, you simply can ask them. I'll be going into this later in the book. Be very clear about the problems your target audience needs you to solve.

If you're not clear on your potential clients' pain points, then it's best to create a survey and find out directly from the source.

On Survey Monkey, you can do this for free. Create a 5 question survey and post a short message on your Facebook page, or even your Instagram page with a caption that reads: "Hey guys, I'm looking to interview 100 people about (insert topic) . This survey will take less than three minutes. If you are a (insert qualifications), and you're willing to answer some quick questions, comment below". Then, send the interview link to everyone who comments. I know that this works because I've done it several times for my own brand research.

Another way to engage with your target audience is to offer free strategy calls to get client information. Offer to give a free 15–20-minute strategy call for the purposes of market research, during which you get on the phone with someone who may be an ideal client for you, and ask him or her questions. Ask the potential client what is challenging him or her. Ask what his or her goals are and ask the potential client what's getting in the way of him or her accomplishing the stated goal. Then, you can use this information to create your products, classes, and services.

Reading comments on social media also can be an amazing source of "inside information". You can find people who have a similar audience or someone who does something similar to you but who has a much larger following. Look in the comments on their posts to see what people are saying and what they need help accomplishing. This is easy research.

You also can find books on Amazon that are similar to the book that you're writing and read the reviews to see what people are saying about them. Look at what people liked about the book and how the book helped them. Pay attention to what people disliked about the book. This may give you insight into the problems and challenges that people may be experiencing and the solutions they are searching for. Now, you can start setting yourself apart from others in your niche. Why should someone come work with *you*? What makes *you* different from anyone else? How can you address their pain points in a way no one else can?

You have to know this, and you have to be able to articulate this to your potential readers. What can you help people do and how will you help them to do it? How long will that take?

Once you're able to articulate this, you will be able to create a benefit statement that tells prospective readers how you can help them, the problem you solve, and the challenge they are facing that you can help them overcome.

The goal here is to help you get as clear as possible. I want to help you write a strategic book that you can use to target your chosen industry and add value to your audience long after you publish your book. Visit www.myppbook.com to access a free resource to help you clarify your niche.

Now, it's time to delve into the value you provide as an author. When you are niching down your topic, here are two more questions to ask yourself:

- For what do I want to be known? (This should be the focus of your book.)
- When people think of me, what's going to come to mind?

For example, when you think of athleticism, you might think of Nike. When you think of healthy foods or health programs, Weight Watchers or LA Fitness may come to mind. When you think of healthy grocery stores, you may think of Whole Foods, Trader Joe's, or another similar chain. The reason these companies are at the forefront of these industries is because they have branded themselves effectively. As an author, you're building a business, so you also have to brand yourself. Ask yourself, *For what do I want to be known? What do I want people to think of when they think of me?*

Have you ever followed someone on social media and then saw them in real life for the first time? After I wrote my first book, social media followers saw me on random occasions out in public, and they'd ask, "Hey, you're the *Twenty Pearls* girl, right?" They'd also ask, "Didn't you write the book, *Twenty Pearls?*" They didn't know anything else about my book or any other parts of the title, but they knew *Twenty Pearls*. Based on my marketing efforts, they knew I had written a book with twenty tips to help women in their twenties grow personally, professionally, spiritually, and mentally. Therefore, when they saw me, they immediately connected me to "Twenty Pearls".

The fifth question to ask yourself is, *What are the values that I hold in high importance?*

These values are going to be reflected in your branding and your book because you're going to talk about them at some point.

The sixth question is, *How can my values and personal experiences become part of my brand positioning?* This is where authenticity comes into play as you share your morals, values, character, and beliefs with your audience.

You speak about these topics in your book and your branding further communicates them. You don't have to hide or try to create an image that's not true to who you are or cannot be held up. Be yourself. In your book, you will share your values and experiences, so this needs to be reflected in your marketing, too.

When people see you, what is it that you represent? It's okay if you turn people off because that's what effective branding does. Your messaging and values are going to attract the people who want what you have to offer. In the same way, they're going to repel those who are not in alignment with your message. Therefore, you must understand that not everybody is going to like you. There are going to be some people who will unfollow you or dislike your promotions—that is absolutely okay.

Do you know why? It's okay because they're not going to buy your book anyway. It means that they are not your ideal reader or client; they are not your audience. That's the purpose of marketing and messaging. That's the purpose of niching your topic all the way down. That's also the purpose of being specific, and that's the purpose of authenticity.

Let's consider former President Donald Trump, for example. Despite your personal opinions and political affiliation, he is a genius at marketing. The reason he was so polarizing is that he knew what he wanted to be known for, and he spoke shamelessly about it.

Now, I'm not saying that you should use his tactics or strategies, but I want you to look at what he did to become the topic of conversations. When he was actively on social media, he had two audiences: those who absolutely loved him and those who absolutely hated him.

The reason he's so polarizing is that he knew what he wanted to be known for. Prior to being banned on social media, he shared his values every single day on Twitter, on the news, and on any platform to anybody who would listen. He allowed his values and experiences to become a part of his image and brand.

Therefore, he attracted those who aligned with his messaging and core values. At the same time, he strongly repelled those who did not. He didn't have lukewarm followers. You either loved him or hated him.

Now, let's consider you.

How can you be your authentic self? How can you share your values, personal experiences, and expertise and align them with your topic as you write your book and grow your brand? You do this by identifying your ULEs, matching each one with a specific chapter in your book, and sharing your authentic truth.

Align Your Book with Your End Goal

Now, it's time to align your book with your end goal. This is where you want to begin with the end in mind. Remember, you want to write a book that doesn't simply tell your story; you want to write a book that is going to put you in the optimal position to obtain additional opportunities.

If this process is stretching you a bit because now you're going in a slightly different direction than you may have been headed previously, you are on the right track!

It's not enough to just write a book. You want to write a Bankable Book ™ that you can continue to monetize beyond the bookshelf and initial release date. This is where you're going to delve deeper.

An effective way to align your book with your end goal is to research your industry within the city in which you live. I'd advise you to not look nationally at first. My suggestion is that you begin growing your brand locally and become a local hometown hero before spreading your wings. Once you understand your city, then you can expand to your state, followed by other states. The great thing about it is that all of this can be done with a simple Google search! Look for conferences, organizations, events, schools, and school programs related to your industry.

If you are writing a book for single mothers, look up conferences for single mothers, non-profit organizations, or clubs for single mothers in your city. What are some events, branches, or other local gatherings that have been created for single mothers? Are there school events or programs for this particular audience? What type of media coverage has been released about single mothers? Is there a national day of observance for single moms? Conduct a Google search and see what you find. Then, determine how you can align your message with the needs of the organization, and brainstorm content you can create for that audience. Visit www.myppbook.com to access a free resource to help you align your topic with organizations and events who need what you have.

Research other authors who have written a book similar to your topic and have been featured on the news in your city. On what radio stations has he or she been featured? What were they invited on the platforms to discuss? Determine why these organizations, conferences, events, and schools needed their message- and why they need your message. Most importantly, how can your book help these audiences?

Also, consider events held and hosted by the local commerce and business groups in your city, because they each have their own evening meetups or monthly lunches. Consider how you can align yourself with these events, attract potential readers, and generate leads into your audience through them. It's important for you to learn this information so you can be aware of the possibilities that exist for you and understand where your audience is.

While you're conducting market research on different authors in your industry, this is also an opportunity for you to look at their websites and see what kinds of events they attend as speakers. Although the event may not be located in your city, it will give you an idea of similar events you can research. You don't know what you don't know, but you'll learn what you don't know by conducting research and learning about the opportunities that exist.

This might all feel a bit overwhelming but remember that you're not going to start reaching out to organizations yourself right at this moment. The groundwork you are establishing now is going to prepare you for success later when your book is published. However, you can begin building relationships now, which is especially important if you have the desire to speak. If you know that you eventually want to speak at certain events and conferences and position yourself to sell bulk orders of books, then you need to begin building relationships now by showing your face, connecting with others, and enhancing their organization.

Hopefully, you're beginning to understand that the value you provide extends way beyond the book itself. By now, you're starting to conduct research to help you align your book with the end goal, organizations, conferences, events, schools, and people. Soon, you will be able to go into venues and contribute to their organizational goals and vision, speak, share about your book, and build relationships with others in your industry. Through your book, you will change lives!

Authorpreneur Interview

Name: Atoya Follins
Business Name: A Follins LLC
Website URL: www.atoyafollins.com
Social Media Links: https://instagram.com/atoyafollins

Tell us about your book: The name of my book is Girl, You Have Purpose. I officially launched my book the night before International Women's Day in 2020. I'm a girl's girl and love to see women empowered in life and in business, so the timing of my launch was very exciting for me.

Who is your book for and why do they need it? My book is for the woman over the age of 35 who has given so much of herself to all of the roles that she plays in life that she's forgotten to nurture the purpose that God has given her. Girl, You Have Purpose is needed to show women how to tap into themselves and align with their gifts and their divine assignments.

What did you learn about yourself during your writing and publishing process? Even though the intent of writing my book was to help women discover purpose in their lives, the process allowed me to become more clear on my own.

What advice would you offer to professionals who desire to write a book? My advice to any professional wanting to write a book is to DO IT! Packaging your knowledge in this way will lead to open doors, rooms, and tables that you had no idea had been waiting on you to show up.

Anything else you'd like to share? Becoming an author can be an intimidating process. You'll think of every reason why you can't write your book. Don't sit with these thoughts for long. Focus on the one reason that you can and keep going.

Chapter 3

Embrace Your Voice & Share Your Story

If you are writing a book that contains a lot of personal information, you may be wondering how much of your story you should tell.

What details should you share? How do you go about writing the parts of your story that involve others?

Well, the first thing you should do is determine the overall point of your book. Everything you write must be aligned with the end goal, so I want you to answer the following questions:

1. Why did you decide to write your book? Remember, your purpose has to be about more than just sharing your story and simply talking about what has happened to you.
2. Who is your book for? I want you to visualize one person in your mind. If you were writing to only one person, who would it be? How old is he or she? Is the person a male or a female? What are his or her experiences? What kind of life has he or she had that puts him or her in a position of needing to read your book? (Your book can't be for everyone, or for all people).

3. By the time the reader reaches the end of your book, what will they learn? What is their epiphany? How do you want your book to impact and affect them?
4. What problem does your book solve? What is the one problem that your reader has in their life or business that they need help with?

It's important to realize that we aren't referring to your friends and family who are mainly going to purchase your book because they want to support you. This one person is your ideal reader, and he or she is struggling with something. This 'something' is the reason he or she needs your book. He or she doesn't *want* your book; this person *needs* your book. Got it? Good! Let's continue to peel back the layers of the onion a bit. Begin with the end in mind before you write a single word.

Once you've identified the problem that your book solves, and once you've identified the number one "aha" moment your reader will have by the time he or she reaches the end of your book, you need to determine how many chapters it will take for you to get to the point and provide the solution.

This is where you must assess where your reader currently is versus where they need to be. By this, I mean that you have to determine the challenges your reader is facing right now (before they read your book) as well as the solution they are looking for and desire to obtain.

Reflect on the following questions:

- How many chapters will it take for you to solve the problem for the reader?
- What challenges does your reader have at the moment (as it relates to your topic)?
- What does he or she need help with urgently?
- What is he or she struggling with at this very minute?

The answers to these questions will provide an indication to you of the solutions your book can provide.

- What is the number one transformation that you want your reader to have?
- How does the transformation look?
- What will your readers be able to accomplish in their minds, spirits, emotions, life or business after reading your book?

This is where you must determine the main factors and learning points you need to know in order to transform your readers from where they are to where they want and need to be. This is where you make the shift from writing a book that *you* want to write and telling your story to writing a book that your *reader* needs and wants.

To do this, you need to share information in a way that is going to help your reader attain their desired goal by the end of your book.

Consider the number of chapters it will take for you to provide information that will help your readers receive the transformation they need. Is it going to take 10 chapters? Is it going to take 12 chapters? Is it going to take seven chapters to get your readers from where they are to where they want and need to be? I want you to pause right now and establish your end point. How many chapters are going to be in your book? How long does your book need to be for the reader to get the result, breakthrough, and transformation that they are seeking?

Making this decision and utilizing this strategy will help you avoid the attempt to put your entire life story or professional experience into a book. Visit www.myppbook.com to access a free resource to help you outline your chapters.

Your entire life and years of experience will not fit into one book. If you try to incorporate too much detail to your manuscript, it may make for a boring book!

This is why you must become focused on the one thing- the one outcome- your readers need. You must concentrate on specific lessons and experiences that you will share to help your readers get from where they are to where they want and need to be. Oftentimes, these lessons and experiences will stem from a personal experience that you have had at some point and time in your life or career.

Once you outline your chapters using the free resources located at www.myppbook.com, you will have completed the first framework for your book. This is the beginning of your outline, and we are going to develop it further as we move through this book. However, even though your book may look as if it is starting to take form, do not start writing your book just yet! Instead, stay focused on these exercises; they will help you sculpt your story as we go. These strategies will help you develop the solid foundation and direction you need in order to complete your book in a short period of time.

As a rule of thumb, you should aim to include a minimum of 100 pages in your book. Now, 100 pages is approximately 20,000 words in a 5.5 x 8.5 size book. For reference, this book is 5.5 (width) x 8.5 (length).

Here's a quick guideline if you want your book to have 25,000 words:

- 12 chapters: 2,083 words per chapter
- 10 chapters: 2,500 words per chapter
- 7 chapters: 3,571 words per chapter

Chances are high that each chapter **will not** have the exact same number of words. Some chapters may have more or fewer words than others. Don't stress yourself out about trying to make each chapter the same length, or try to stick to this breakdown like it is a law. Again, this is a simple guide to help you reach your page count goals.

If you do not want to write 2,000-3,000 words per chapter but still want 100 pages in your book, one hack is to write 1,500 words per chapter. Then, at the end of each chapter, you can include reflection questions, recap main points, and/or insert lined pages for journaling.

Another option is to include quotes, poems, case studies, client success stories, and testimonials in and throughout your book. Again, you can include this additional content at the end of each chapter. These are some of the strategies you can use to boost your page count without having to increase the word count and modify the content in each chapter. Get creative and think about your ideal reader. What content does he or she need? And what do they respond to the best?

Next, as you move toward beginning to write your book, make the determination to own your story. Stop comparing your story and journey to the story or journey of others. I don't want you to be ashamed, embarrassed, scared, or fearful to release your book to the masses. The world needs your voice.

Yes, you will see other people writing books. You will see other people promoting their products and services, but recognize that your expertise is not another author's expertise. Your voice is not that author's voice. Even if the topic is similar, the perspective and strategies that you offer may be totally different than the insight of someone else. Yes, you may see others doing the same kind of work you're doing or providing books and services in the same industry, but they will not do it the same way that you will because your **voice only belongs to you**.

For instance, did you ever know two different math teachers in school who taught the same subject? You may have had one teacher you couldn't understand at all, and who inadvertently made you feel like math just wasn't your thing. However, across the hall was another math teacher who you went to after school for tutorial because they broke the concepts down and made them much easier for you to understand. This is a perfect example of two teachers teaching the exact same subject, but their methods of instruction, which impact effectiveness, were completely different. The same applies to you when it comes to your book, so if you're concerned about the market being saturated, don't be.

Here's something else to consider when you start writing your book: you must eliminate the shackles of other people's opinions and be authentic in sharing your story. Yes, people will talk and have opinions about your book, but that's a great thing! For a start, it's free publicity for you. Here's some other food for thought: If you were doing nothing and weren't making a greater impact in the world, then no one would have anything to say. When people talk about you, others are going to pay more attention to you. Don't hold back because you're afraid of offending others, and don't cap your calling because of the criticisms of onlookers. Eliminate the shackles of other people's opinions.

As you push past your fears, keep in mind that sharing your story is your responsibility. You have not had your experiences so that you can keep your wisdom and insights to yourself. Share your lessons learned and help the next person. Your story is like a mantle; you have a responsibility to use it wisely and courageously by sharing it with the world. Additionally, your story is your stairwell to six and seven-figure success. Having the courage to share your story can open up opportunities for you to create multiple streams of revenue beyond your book through professional speaking, courses, coaching programs, and more.

I am often asked, "How much of my story should I tell? How much is too much?"

First, let's remember to keep the focus of your content on your experiences and the lessons you've learned as a result of your experiences. You don't want to write from the role of a victim even if you were victimized at some point in your story. **Instead, you must write with your reader in mind.** To determine how much of your personal story you should tell, examine your ULEs. ULE is an acronym for Unique Life Experiences. These unique life experiences are the core experiences that became defining moments in your life.

At the beginning of this chapter, you decided how many chapters you were going to include in your book. Using your initial chapter outline, you're going to align a ULE with each chapter. By laying your story out in this way, your focus will be clear, and the ULE "roadmap" will prevent you from trying to tell too much of your story. It will also prevent you from telling the parts that aren't essential to the overall purpose of your book.

Focusing on your ULEs allows you the opportunity to pull multiple stories from your unique experiences.

For example, say I wanted to talk about my college experience and the guy I dated for three years. Yes, I could share about my overall experience with him and intimate details of our relationship. However, that would be overload Plus, I wouldn't want to write a book where the primary topic is an expired relationship. Alternatively, I can share specific instances and moments - individual stories - that I experienced during that chapter of my life, such as the situations with him that taught me how to set boundaries in relationships, how to determine whether someone is good for you, and how to have the courage to pursue your goals despite what those closest to you say or think.

The ULE method will serve as a framework for your chapters and help guide your writing to ensure you stay on track. Visit www.myppbook.com to access a free resource to help you map out your own ULEs.

This strategy will help you incorporate your personal experiences into your book without your book being overloaded with sensitive or extraneous information that does not lead the reader to the intended outcome. Using the ULE method, you will avoid writing a book that only focuses on your story because, remember, you're writing your book to solve a problem for the reader.

Now, to answer the age old question: how much of your story should you tell?

First, remember to take the focus off yourself.

Second, identify the particular situations and examples you will pull from the ULEs that you want to share in each chapter. Remember that the ULEs you share must relate to what you're talking about in the chapter. This is going to help you to stay focused.

Third, make sure you acknowledge your role. Acknowledge what you learned from the situations and experiences and ask yourself, "What is the point of me sharing this?" Then ask, "What will the reader learn from me sharing this experience, and how can I position and frame this experience in a way that will help the reader?"

Finally, determine whether the experience you desire to share aligns with the goal of the chapter. Since your book is solving a problem, each chapter should help the readers arrive with a solution to their problem or achieve a transformation by the time they reach the end of your book. This means that you must write intentionally with a goal in mind for each chapter. Visit www.myppbook.com to access a free resource to help you map and outline the focus and goals for each chapter of your book.

Your reader should learn something from each part of your book, so the experience you desire to share should align with the goal of the chapter and the overall objective of the book. If what you are writing does not accomplish a specific objective, you probably need to leave it out.

Chapter 4

Organizing Your Content

So far, you've learned about the mindset and attitude you should develop in order for your writing and publishing process to be a success. You've also learned the number of words required to write a 7, 10, or 12-chapter book. By this time, you should have decided how many chapters you're going to include in your book.

You've also taken the time to niche your topic and audience, as well as align your topic with different industries. By now, you have a clear idea of exactly what the focus of your book needs to be and who its audience needs to be.

In chapter three, you identified your ULEs, or your unique learning experiences. You also drafted the first framework for your outline, which means that you have identified the main talking points in your book that are going to help your reader get from where they are to their desired outcome.

It's now time to plan your writing even further and develop your outline fully. Visit www.myppbook.com to receive a free resource to access the Organized Outline Framework and develop a detailed outline of your manuscript.

Planning Your Content

Before you write anything, you must plan your writing by creating an outline. This outline will include your chapter title, main topics, subtopics, supporting details, and closing point for each chapter. Mapping out your chapters using main topics, subtopics, and supporting details will help you determine the content to include in your chapters. Visit www.myppbook.com to access the Organized Outline Framework to help you develop a fully detailed outline of your manuscript.

Your subtopics are the specific touchpoints you desire to discuss in your chapter. Your supporting details may consist of examples, personal stories, dialogue, and case studies. Close out your chapter with an empowering or encouraging message and a call to action for your reader. Then, repeat this strategy for each chapter in your book.

Authorpreneur Interview

Name: Tracie Johnson
Website URL: www.traciejohnson.com
Social Media Links: FaceBook- Tracie Johnson
Instagram- @pennedbytracie
Twitter- pennedbytracie

Tell us about your book: Dear Self, Please Forgive Me is a woman's guide to self love and self forgiveness. It is a tool that was created to assist women in learning how to let go of the past. This book forces a woman to examine herself. It shows her how to dig deep, how to accept accountability for her past hurts, encouraging her to press forward in love and forgiveness of herself. It's full of affirmations to show a woman that she is more than she's allowing herself to be.

Who is your book for and why do they need it? Dear Self is for the woman who constantly finds herself in a place of hopelessness, not knowing if she is coming or going. It's for the woman who constantly walks around in heaviness because she feels she can't be accepted. This book is for the woman who constantly criticizes everything about herself, seeking validation just to feel recognized. Dear Self is for the woman who is ready to live, love, and be free.

What did you learn about yourself during your writing and publishing process? While writing, I learned there were a lot of past issues and hurts I'd placed upon myself that kept me from loving the woman in the mirror. I learned that in order to get off the bed of suicide, I needed to heal from the inside out, not the outside in. I learned that I was responsible for my own peace and happiness. I found out how bold and powerful I truly was. During the publishing process, I discovered a new level of patience and perseverance buried deep within.

What advice would you offer to professionals who desire to write a book? Perhaps you find yourself with a desire to write, wanting to share your expertise in your field and don't know which way to go, or even where to begin. I advise you to run expeditiously to Jasmine. God has given her the tools and the know-how to help pull that book out of you! She's passionate about what she does and I've seen first-hand how her strategies and techniques have helped not just me, but hundreds of other men and women. Her program guarantees to work, IF you put in the work!

Anything else you'd like to share? Remember to Live, Love, and Be FREE!

Chapter 5:

Writing Your Book

It's now time to write your book! To help you remain consistent, dedicate a period of time each day to writing. This should be, at the very least, 15 minutes per day, but I encourage you to block out more than that if you are able. For a more aggressive approach, you can spend one hour writing every day for the next two to three weeks or until you've completed your book.

However, if you focus on completing one chapter per day as opposed to one hour per day as suggested, this will allow you to have a measurable goal you can reach during each writing session. Before you know it, you'll be done, and you can finish writing your book in less than a month.

This is the exact same method I used to write my first book. I wrote every single day for about 14 days. Because I was so immersed in the process, I began to double up and, at times, found myself writing two chapters per day.

In this way, I was able to write a 20-chapter book in about two weeks after struggling with it for 10 years.

Here are a few things to remember:

1. While you are writing, do not talk "at" your reader. Make sure that you are relaxed and write as if you are having a conversation with a friend. This means that

while you are actually typing, it is best not to worry about grammar. This is neither the time for you to be the grammar police nor is it the time for your book to be perfect. There will be time for refining later. Right now, let go of control.
2. This version of your book is called your rough draft, and it's called your rough draft for a reason. It's a draft, and it's going to be rough. This is not your final published version. The purpose of your rough draft is for you to get out all of the ideas that are inside you. For this reason, it's similar to an organized brain dump, and likely will be rough at first.
3. Type your book in Google Docs. Don't write with pen and paper, or else you will find yourself having to do double the work down the line. We'll talk more about this later.
4. Please, do not erase everything and start over.
5. Do not keep rereading and rewriting to try to perfect your manuscript. By all means, do not try to edit your book as you go. Editing is not your job, even if you are a naturally strong writer.

Your job as the author is to write the book and get your ideas and stories from the inside of your head to the outside world. Tell your story.

Any time you start to feel like you are hitting a wall, I want you to ask yourself , "If I was sitting across the table talking to my ideal mentee, how would that conversation go?

How would I talk to him or her? What would I say to him or her? What language would I use? How would I connect with him or her?"

That's the same frame of mind that you should adopt as you are writing your book. Your book should be written in a conversational, relatable tone, so just write it. Don't try to sound extremely proper or perfect. It is not the time for that. Right now, you need to say what it is you need to say. Release your words and don't hold back.

Essentially, this is an organized brain dump of your ideas. Using your outline as your guide, you must make sure that you write down and share all the information and ideas that come to mind.

Personally, I have always been a strong writer, and I was a language arts teacher for 12 years. Imagine my stress when I was trying to write my first book! I literally questioned, reread, and rewrote everything I typed because I was trying to make my first draft into a perfect masterpiece as I was writing.

After hitting a brick wall for 10 years, I realized that the perfect masterpiece is the book that gets published. I serve and help no one by keeping my story to myself. Allowing a spirit of perfectionism to procrastinate my progress, my destiny, and calling was selfish.

Who am I helping by staying stuck because my words don't sound right to *me?*

I am helping absolutely no one.

I realized that if I really wanted to help others, I had to take the focus off myself, make my readers the focus, and allow my editors to do the heavy lifting of perfecting the content.

Tools to Use

If you are trying to write your book by hand using pen and paper, stop it immediately. Stop it now, I say! This method is old and outdated, not to mention the document must be provided electronically to the editors. You don't want to put yourself in a position in which you are doing double work by having to type your document after you handwrite it.

I strongly advise you to type your book using a system such as Google Docs because it is cloud-based, which means you can access your file from any device, anywhere. That way, in the event of theft or damage to your computer or files, your manuscript will still exist untouched, unharmed, and unfazed.

Trust me, I've lost plenty of manuscripts. I've also had clients who completed their manuscripts but lost their files due to their computers crashing. Thank goodness that I had backup files!

As I write this, one of my first publishing clients comes to mind. I edited my client's book two or three times prior, so she was almost ready for interior design and layout. I was in the middle of working when my computer totally shut off. The hard drive malfunctioned, and I lost all my clients' files. Guess who didn't have the files backed up or stored on a cloud-based system? Me. Yep, that's who.

I had to re-edit not just that one client but ALL my clients' manuscripts from the very beginning. Talk about a major setback! I had to send emails and provide a discount or bonus service in exchange for the extended time needed to complete the projects.

I remember the time a client, who was almost finished writing her book, had her computer stolen. She had to start from scratch—literally, from the first sentence.

You don't want to be placed in a predicament in which you lose all of your content and are forced to write your book over from scratch, so my suggestion is that you use a cloud-based system such as Google Docs, to prevent your manuscript from getting lost or destroyed.

Chapter 6:

Creating Your Money Title

The title of your book either will attract or repel your reader. If you've already titled your book, keep reading because you may learn some new information that may make you rethink your current title.

One mistake I often see independent authors make is that they come up with a title for their book and then try to create content that aligns with the title. When you are writing a book that is solution-oriented, be sure to focus on your content first (because that's what matters most). After you've drafted your content and have a better idea of what your book is going to be about, then you can move forward to create an engaging title that will attract more clients and life-changing opportunities.

Now, you may be thinking, *I already have a title.* I want you to stop and consider whether or not your original title is important to *you, or* whether that title will attract the *reader* who needs your book.

I know that I've repeated it a lot throughout this book, but every decision you make in regard to your book must be made with your reader in mind, and not because it's what YOU desire.

For example, if you're reading this book, *Published and Paid: Write, Self-Publish, and Launch Your Nonfiction Book in*

90 Days or Less, I know that you're interested in learning how to write, self-publish, and make money from a nonfiction book.

Your primary book title should be clear and concise. Ideally, you want to incorporate literary elements such as alliteration into your title. Nonfiction books should always include a subtitle that speaks directly to your audience and the problem that your book solves.

You can also create a play on words with the overall theme or principle of your book. I'm going to show you a few examples of this to help get your creative juices going.

Let's analyze some money-making titles by previous students from my Author Made Easy® Bootcamp coaching program. First, we have Tomasha Suber and her book, *The Six-Figure Solopreneur: Make More Money Without Slaving in Your Business..*

As you can see, her title is clear, direct, and straightforward: *The Six-Figure Solopreneur*. From the title alone, you know that this book is for entrepreneurs who are the only employees in their businesses. You also know that they've either made or are trying to make a six-figure income. The title is catchy because it contains alliteration (repeated use of the "s" sound).

The subtitle for Tomasha's book is "Make More Money Without Slaving in Your Business." Straight away, we know what she's going to be teaching in her book. She's going to teach solopreneurs how to make more money in their businesses in less time and without being a slave (overworked) to their businesses.

Let's look at another winning title.

Jasmyne Reynolds wrote *The Power of Your P: 19 Power Principles to Becoming a Female Boss*. There's a fun play on words there because the first thing that comes to your mind while reading this may be kind of naughty. However, the subtitle clarifies and adds more detail to the title, and you can see that the title is just a play on words.

In her book, *The Power of Your P: 19 Power Principles to Becoming a Female Boss*, Jasmyne talks about the power of your principle. Specifically, she lists 19 power principles for women to win in life.

Finally, let's look at this one: *Don't Let Them Flunk Out: 50 Ways to Get and Stay Connected to Your Students*.

From this title and subtitle, you know that this book is for teachers, and its main purpose is to provide strategies for them to get and stay connected to their students in an effort to decrease the dropout rate. The author, VaLarie Humphrey, is a former assistant principal. She had some struggles in her own academic experience and almost flunked out of school because she had a 1.69 GPA. Despite her challenges in school and struggles with poor grades, she went on to achieve amazing things—one of which was becoming an assistant principal. VaLarie has a real passion for helping disadvantaged students; therefore, her book is a guide for educators to enhance student learning by improving communication and building relationships.

Now, I want you to draft three titles for your book. Even if you've already created a title, I want you to go back to the drawing board and use these strategies:

1. Create a core book title
2. Create a descriptive subtitle that describes your topic and speaks to your audience. Write a specific subtitle that is going to draw your reader in.
3. Then, I want you to select the best of the three. If you are struggling to select the best option, invite your community to provide you with feedback. Share your titles on your social media platforms. You can ask your family and friends which titles they're drawn to the most and why. Whatever you do, make sure you create three titles and select the best of the three.

Next, go on Amazon or browse your home library and select three book covers that you like. Download or scan these covers and upload them to a Google Doc or a Google Drive folder. Let these covers serve as your design inspiration and help you determine how you want your book cover to look. All three of the covers that you've selected are going to have some elements in common that you will likely want included in your book cover design. When it's time for you to get your book cover created, your graphic designer is going to ask you for examples of book covers that you like to help him or her get a feel for your style. You will be able to give this digital folder to your designer, and they will incorporate those common elements into your book cover drafts.

Authorpreneur Interview

Name: Dr. Ramon Goings, EdD
Business Name: The Done Dissertation
Website URL: www.thedonedissertation.com
Social Media Links: www.instagram.com/donedisscoach
www.twitter.com/donedisscoach
www.facebook.com/donedisscoach

Tell us about your book: 14 Secrets to a Done Dissertation: A Guide to Navigating the Dissertation Process and Finishing in Record Time explores fourteen proven strategies that will help doctoral students navigate the dissertation process and finish in record time including:

- How to manage your busy schedule and reclaim your time to finish your dissertation.
- Strategies to overcome perfectionism and procrastination.
- The science and art of selecting a dissertation chair and committee members.
- How to prepare you and your family for your dissertation proposal and final defense

Who is your book for and why do they need it?

14 Secrets to a Done Dissertation: A Guide to Navigating the Dissertation Process and Finishing in Record Time is for the busy doctoral student who is managing a busy home and professional life and has grown frustrated with their lack of progress with their dissertation.

I learned that with just putting in the work and learning a simple process to write my book that Jasmine taught me that I could put together a book that could make an impact on a significant level. Two months after publishing my book 3 university doctoral program made 14 Secrets a required reading. I also learned that as an author we should always look for opportunities to monetize our intellectual property!

What advice would you offer to professionals who desire to write a book?

You have two options. One is that you figure it out yourself and spend a lot of time and money with little results

Two is that you learn Jasmine's proven method to write your book and ensure that it sells. For me, I needed a process that worked and I have literally 10x my initial investment! Additionally, there is just something special about creating one product that you can sell over and over and I would recommend any professional to do this!

Anything else?

If you are stuck working on your dissertation and need support, text me 301-701-2466 and let me know you read this book! I have a special offer for you!

Chapter 7:

Designing Your Book Cover

When it comes to your book cover design, the title of your book should stand out clearly. The subtitle must be prominent enough to be seen, noticed, and read quickly. For reference, visit www.myppbook.com to view model book cover examples of some of the graduates of my Author Made Easy® Bootcamp coaching program.

Prospective readers should be able to view your cover, see the title and subtitle, and know exactly what your book will explore, who the book is written for, and what the readers are going to learn.

As a general rule, your cover should not have any more than three to four colors. Anything more than that runs the risk of being visually overwhelming. The only exception is if the colors you're using on your cover are your brand colors, and you have found a way to incorporate them into your cover strategically without the design overloading the readers' eyes.

Besides the title and subtitle, you also want to ensure that your name and image are clearly visible. The image can be of you, or it can be an image related to the theme or topic of your book. Industry practice is to not include your picture on the front cover of the book unless your image will help to sell the book.

Should You Put Your Picture on the Cover of Your Book?

Unless your picture will help drive more book sales, it's best that your personal image is removed and left off the front cover of your book.

Many bookstores and major retailers will not accept your book if your picture is on the front and you don't have a major audience. Therefore, it's best that your picture is not included unless you already have high visibility and clout. However, your picture can be included on the back of the book in the author biography section. It can also be included inside the book, in an extended about the author section.

Selecting a Book Cover Designer

If you are not a professional designer with a background or experience in design, do not attempt to design your own book cover. Yes, there are free tools online that will allow you to design your own cover. However, when you are writing a Bankable Book™, you want to ensure that you have a cover that is high quality. Most DIY online book cover design tools will result in you creating a sub-par or cheap-looking cover. Trust, that is not the route you should take when you are building a professional brand and using your book to establish yourself as an authority in your field.

Online Design Platforms

There are many ways to get your book cover designed. You can hire a freelancer from a gig site such as 99designs.com, fiverr.com, or upwork.com.

When using a designer from a gig site, you must keep in mind that freelancers often have templates from which they design in order to handle and fulfill the volume of designs that come their way. This means that your cover is likely going to look like someone else's cover in terms of format and design, but it may differ in color and personalization.

Your best option (and my personal preference and recommendation) is to hire a professional graphic designer to work with you and bring your idea to life. A professional designer may charge anywhere from $300 to upwards of $1,500 for an original, customized book cover design. Depending on your price point, budget, and design package, the designer will offer a number of designs for you to choose from with 2-3 rounds of revisions. Any revisions requested outside the contractual amount usually will be an additional fee. It's important to know this before you go into the design process because you will not have an unlimited number of design choices or revisions, so do not expect it. Be sure that you are in a mental space in which you can make a solid decision; otherwise, be willing to pay for additional concepts to be created.

You don't have to get the full cover spread (front cover, spine, and back cover) designed initially, but I do encourage you to get a mock-up 3D design, so you can see what the book is going to look like, and so you can begin taking pre-orders. Even if your cover changes or is not the final version, you can give your early purchasers notification that the book cover design is subject to change. Once your cover design is complete, you actually can go ahead and post the cover online. Inform your audience that your book is going to be officially released within the next 60 to 90 days, and you can begin making money by promoting your book before it is printed.

I want to give you a word of caution about pre-orders. If you receive any money for pre-ordered books, you must operate with integrity and make sure you deliver the product on time. One of the worst things that I've ever seen is an author taking money for a book that they never deliver. If you think that's going to be you or that you have the capacity to do that (take money and never send the books), then you may just want to wait until you have the actual book in your hand.

For some authors, pre-orders serve as an extra push and incentive to finish the book since monies have been collected. You may have the lingering thought, *"People already have purchased copies. I need to follow through and get it done."*

Go ahead and get your cover designed. This helps make your goal a reality and brings it within reach. Visit www.myppbook.com to receive a free resource to gain access to your book cover design checklist, and see examples of high quality cover designs.

Chapter 8:
The Revision Process

After the first draft of your book is complete, it's time to revise your writing. During the revision phase, you must read and review your writing with the goal of improving your content. Remember, you're not seeking perfection. The objective is to clean up and modify obvious errors such as spelling, punctuation, capitalization, run-on sentences, and fragments. During the revision phase, you will need to rewrite and fill in any gaps. You will need to revise your writing before you send your manuscript to an editor. After you have finished writing, make sure you read over your manuscript once or twice and revise it.

Now, this is not the time for you to get stuck and continue adding content. Remember, don't overthink things or allow doubt to set in. Reread your manuscript from cover to cover once, maybe twice, just to make sure that you correct the obvious errors and add content wherever details are lacking. Then, send your manuscript to your editor because the editor is the one who's going to work the magic. Your editor will bring your book to life, so leave the heavy lifting to him or her. Let your editor do what you are paying him or her to do. Your editor is going to read your book, tell you what changes you need to make, and why you need to make them.

This is also why I previously mentioned that the time that you're writing is not the time for you to perfect your story. Your editor is the one who's going to perfect it and provide suggestions for you to enhance your content and help you bring all of your ideas together.

Avoid the urge to keep adding content outside of what the editor suggests. In order to simplify the process, you only should add what you need to incorporate in your book. I suggest that you wait on the editor to give you feedback because he or she will tell you how to modify your manuscript. The editor also will tell you what content to remove as well as what content to rearrange and why you should change it. Trust yourself and don't doubt the work you've completed up until now. Remember, it will be necessary for you to add some content to your book. However, you don't want to add so much content that you start going off topic, confusing yourself, or self-sabotaging yourself by overthinking and not finishing what you started. Therefore, I can't stress this enough: save the heavy lifting for your editor.

When it's time for you to have your book edited, it is worth paying someone to do a quality job . There's no point in you stressing over the revisions and making sure that your manuscript is perfect. Do what you can and let your editor do the rest.

Preparing for the Editing Process

Before you go into the editing process, you should be

informed and know what to expect. Many authors expect editors to be ghostwriters, but there's a stark difference between the two.

Please don't assume that your editor is going to rewrite your book. Your editor will review your book and will advise you on the corrections that you need to make. Then, it's your responsibility to review the suggestions and correct your manuscript. When you pay an editor to edit your manuscript, you cannot and should not assume that your editor is going to draft your final manuscript and finalize all of your edits. Your editor is going to do what you're paying him or her to do, which is check your structure, grammar, and writing style. It's your job to review their suggestions, ask questions when you have them, and either accept or reject their suggested edits. You are a partner with your editor during the editing process, and as your editor fulfills their role, you have a responsibility to fulfill yours as well.

Editing actually can be the most expensive part of the writing and publishing process, but it's important because you don't want to publish a book that's poorly edited. A book that's full of mistakes, including grammatical and punctuation errors, is going to reflect poorly on you and your brand. You're not going to be able to sell the book if people can't read it, or if they open it and see tons of errors staring them in the face. Good editing is a cost of doing business, so it has to be a cost that you are ready and willing to pay.

Gig sites often provide fast, easy, and cheap editing services. The cheapest is not always the best, so it's important to hire an editor who knows the conventions of the language in which you are writing.

There are generally three types of editing:

- copy editing
- developmental editing
- proofreading

In order to have a thorough edit performed on your book, you will need all three types of edits. Copy editing checks for spelling, punctuation, capitalization, and grammatical errors. Developmental editing checks for unity, coherence, and the logical flow of ideas. Even if you think that you are a strong writer, the content you've written may not reach the reader in the way that you've intended. This is why you must hire an experienced editor to make sure your content and voice are conveyed clearly.

Proofreading occurs during the final stage of the editing process. This is when your final draft or proof copy is reviewed for any final changes that you may need to make prior to sending your book to print.

Editing Tools

Grammarly has many useful purposes as does Hemingway Editor, which is a free resource. You can also check out ProWritingAid. If you decide to use ProWritingAid, you'll have to search for it as an add-on extension within

Google Docs and download it to your account. You can Google the instructions easily or go through the help section of Google Docs to figure out how to do this. These are just some of the self-editing tools that can help you prepare a professional manuscript. You may find others as you search!

While the DIY approach doesn't achieve the same level of detail as a professional human editor, these tools will get the basic job done. However, my professional opinion is that, even if you use these tools, you always need a human editor. Always.

You can find an editor in your network, through referrals, or on Fiverr or Upwork.com.

Hiring an Editor

When you are looking for an editor, you will find that most professional editors will charge a set fee per word or per page. Most professional editors will charge per word because the per page word count can vary depending on the font size and style used to type the content, which can inadvertently increase the page count of your manuscript which can inadvertently increase the page count of your manuscript if a larger font size is used.. Therefore, most professional editors will charge you per word. There are some editors who charge by the hour; however, in my opinion, this can be difficult to track and ensure that the editor is making the best use of his or her time.

Before you approach an editor, you need to know the final word count of your entire document, including your back cover synopsis if you want your synopsis reviewed and edited as well. Your word count also includes your table of contents, introduction, dedication, conclusion, etc. Your editing quote should consist of all content from cover to cover, word for word. Generally, editing pricing ranges from $0.018 per word to $0.05 or more per word for a professional editor.

Questions to Ask Your Editor

A Published and Paid™ author is an informed author. Don't blindly hire an editor (even if they do have excellent reviews). To help you have a successful and enjoyable editing experience, here are a few questions you should ask your editor prior to hiring them:

- What does my service include?
- What type of editing will be performed on my manuscript?
- How many rounds of edits are included with my payment?
- Do you have an editing agreement (contract)?
- What's the full cost?
- When can I expect to receive the deliverable?
- What's the policy if the manuscript isn't returned to me fully edited by the date identified on the editing agreement?
- Do you have terms for cancellations and refunds? If so, what are they?

Your editing agreement needs to include all of this information. If it doesn't, you can provide an editing agreement yourself that covers this information in detail. Whatever you do, make sure the agreement protects you and your interests to prevent an editor from taking advantage of you. While you can find editing agreements and templates online or by conducting a Google search, I highly recommend that you have a contractual agreement prepared or reviewed by an attorney who specializes in intellectual property.

Your Responsibility in the Editing Process

Even when you hire an editor and pay them, you always need to review your edits. I touched on this previously, but I can't tell you the number of times I've seen authors hire an editor and blindly trust them. These authors never reviewed their edits, so they went on to publish books filled with errors. Unfortunately, they didn't discover this until after their first order of books had been printed. Review your manuscript after each round of edits. Be sure not to review the edits passively by mass accepting all edits and never reading or reviewing your manuscript. It's imperative that you pay extremely close attention to the suggestions and direction that the editor is providing. Be sure to implement what the editor is asking you to do.

If the editor is telling you to change some of the content, then you need to change some of the content. If the editor is telling you that certain sections need more developments or details, you should review those sections of your book, take time to develop the content and provide more details. Refrain from "accepting all edits" or ignoring your editor's suggestions. You actually have to take your time and make the revisions and corrections the editor recommends.

If you fail to review the edits and make the suggested revisions, your final printed book will be full of errors. If this happens, it will be your fault for not doing your due diligence.

As a self-published author, you have full creative control and are responsible for the project management of your book. Regardless of whom you hire, your book is your responsibility, and your final product will be a reflection of your effort.

Proofing and Printing Your Book

Publishing your book is not just about putting it on Amazon. First, you're going to receive a proof copy of your book to review. After you review and approve the initial proof, you'll have to print a full order of your books. Be sure to proofread your advanced reader copy before you order hundreds of copies! Proofreading the proof copy allows you to catch any lingering mistakes in your book before you order hundreds or thousands of copies of your book.

You can also print or order extra copies of your book for a roundtable reading with friends so you can receive more feedback and make final corrections. Many eyes make light work.

After you proof your book and approve it, then you're ready to go to print.

You can find a local print company or use an online company such as Amazon, Lulu, or another online platform to print your books. You will have to select the trim size of your book, the cover type (paperback or hardcover, glossy or matte finish), and the paper type (for example, cream or white paper).

Protecting Your Work

You're also going to need to file and register your copyright, International Standard Book Number (ISBN), which is the barcode that goes on the back of your book cover, as well as your Library of Congress Control Number (LCCN). After all those steps, you'll spend time marketing, pre-launching, launching, distributing, and finally selling your book. We'll discuss this in detail in Chapter 9.

Websites to Visit:

- United States Copyright Office- www.copyright.gov - register your work for copyright. Prices range from $35 and up.
- International Standard Book Number- https://isbn.org - secure your ISBN and barcode for your book. Prices range from $125 and up.
- Library of Congress Control Number-

www.loc.gov - allows your book to be placed in and throughout libraries in the United States. Free registration.

Authorpreneur Interview

Name: Dr. Juantisa Hughes
Business Name: Hughes Alliance, LLC
Website URL: https://juantisahughes.com
Social Media Links:
Personal FB Page: https://www.facebook.com/jxhughes
Business FB Page: https://www.facebook.com/profile.php?id=100063466571696
Instagram: https://www.instagram.com/juantisahughes/
Twitter: https://twitter.com/JuantisaHughes

Tell us about your book. Who is your book for and why do they need it?

The title of my book is *I Think I Made a Mistake: How to Restore Your Marriage (Even If You're on the Brink of Divorce).* It is for anyone experiencing hardships in their marriage, contemplating separation, or planning to file for divorce. Even if the divorce papers have already been filed and the court date has been set, this book is a must read. For the person who desires to be married, this book will definitely help as they prepare for the many things the marriage covenant may bring to, stir up within, and reveal from them. From substance abuse to infidelity, blended families, financial strain, and in-law involvement ... I THINK I MADE A MISTAKE teaches how to identify triggers, what real forgiveness requires, and the Believer's keys to restoration.

What did you learn about yourself during your writing and publishing process?

During the writing and publishing process I learned that I have plenty of books in me but without the proper guidance I would not have been able to birth the first one. As I wrote my book, many new perspectives arose because I was growing and healing in new ways during the process. It was therapeutic. As I published my book, I realized that the intricate steps I had to follow were stretching me to become the business woman I needed to be. I now understand my business worth and my book's true value.

What advice would you offer to professionals who desire to write a book?

Your book is your brand. If written and published properly, it will open doors to a world of opportunities. So, don't cut corners. Invest in yourself and learn the tools to organize your thoughts, center your writing, and produce a quality publication that will impact the masses.

Chapter 9

Marketing, Promotions, and Sales

If you don't take the time to properly market and promote your book, your sales efforts will be in vain. Marketing begins the moment you begin writing your book- not the moment you are ready to sell your book.

BRANDING

Branding includes much more than having a website designed, and it's more than having business cards created. Branding is not limited to your company colors and your promotional and marketing items. Branding consists of more than having a logo designed, and how many social media followers you have. Those elements are a *part* of branding, but branding as a whole is a much bigger picture than any one of those aspects. I'm telling you this because I've worked with so many authors who feel like they have to run out and get a website and a logo, and their inability to decide on a color palette stalls their progress. As all this time goes by, they're not selling books or generating any revenue, and it's all because of a color palette and website. To be honest, most of the things people think is "branding" are things you don't even need to make money.

Proper branding matters because it dictates what people say about you when you're not in the room. Branding allows someone to make an educated decision about your business and whether they want to work with you or purchase a book from you. If your branding and messaging resonates with them, they'll make this decision based on your expertise, your consistency, and the quality of your service. When someone sees you or your social media profiles, they may reach out to people with whom you say that you've worked with or contact you directly with inquiries and for more details. Regardless of their actions, people will develop an immediate impression about you after coming in contact with your brand and messaging on any platform.

The main way to create an authentic brand is to be who it is you say you are. That means if you help female domestic violence victims heal themselves and create a new life, then we should see you doing that. We should see you with relevant non-profit organizations. We should see you in the women's shelters. We should see you hosting seminars and working with these women. A lot of people "brand themselves" with titles such as : "I'm a speaking coach" or "I am a personal development coach" or "I am a women's empowerment speaker." However, at the same time, we often never see the fruits of the person being who they claim to be. We may hear people calling themselves one thing or another, but we never see them working in that space. Therefore, no one can vouch for them except themselves! There goes your credibility down the drain.

However, when you are who you say you are, and you begin to leave clues of your work and results, people will start bringup your name, refer others to you, and give you testimonials, important social proof, and credibility.

Another way to brand yourself is by building a relationship with your audience. This is an absolute must. Now, I've focused a lot of my marketing efforts in the online marketing sphere, and I initially used organic marketing methods (such as instructional video content) to grow my business. I moved forward to help my clients grow their brands and businesses using these methods and helped them start generating revenue online. Building and cultivating relationships is one of the main ways my clients were able to increase their success.

Here are three concrete strategies to build an authentic relationship with your audience:

#1. *Live Streaming*

One of the easiest ways to increase your brand visibility is by live streaming. At the time of writing this, live streaming has now been around about eight years, and it is still a fairly new concept. One of the first social media platforms to offer live stream video was Periscope. With the press of a button, you could instantly reach people all over the world who were interested in listening to you speak on topics they found interest in. After Periscope's popularity, Facebook created its Facebook Live feature, followed by Instagram, YouTube, Twitter and LinkedIn, which added the video live stream feature shortly after Periscope's success. All these platforms are quite recent developments, which is more of a reason for you to jump on the live streaming bandwagon before it gets too crowded.

Once you live stream consistently on platforms such as Facebook, Instagram, and YouTube Live, it will help you to showcase your expertise. Believe it or not, people will start looking out for you, especially if you're showing up consistently with engaging topics and valuable content. One of the ways that I started building my brand in earnest was by live streaming once a week on the same day and at the same time. I created a weekly show during which I would put up a reminder post at least 12 to 24 hours ahead of my live stream to let people know what I'd be talking about and what time to show up online, and I'd stick to my streaming schedule *no matter what*. Don't let a trusting audience down!

If you've ever thought of being interviewed on podcasts, public speaking or other publicity options, live streaming is also a great way to practice these skills because you have an opportunity to broadcast yourself regularly to an audience. Live streaming gives you an opportunity to hone your presentation skills. You can refine your speaking skills too, because you're able to speak via a virtual live stream instead of being physically present in a room with others. Live streaming is the perfect way to practice for bigger events and bigger successes from the comfort of your living room or home office.

In 2020, the app Clubhouse introduced audio-based live streaming, which shifted marketing even more.

Audio-based live streaming is extremely convenient because you don't have to fine tune your appearance or sit in front of a computer. Plus, it allows the option for you to engage in a live group conversation with your listeners. As long as you have a strong phone signal and quiet background, you can participate in an audio-based livestream any time you desire.

Now, I want to challenge you. If you are not live streaming or if you have never live streamed, go ahead and start today. Even if it's just a 5-minute chat to your followers on Instagram, start reaching out to your audience! Which brings us to my next point.

#2. *Connect With Your Audience*

Another way to increase your visibility is to make connections with your audience. This is done by sharing personal stories and experiences to which others can relate, which helps them build a connection with you as a brand. Connection marketing means that you have to allow yourself to be a little bit vulnerable. You're not revealing all your personal business, but you do need to be willing to share personal information that relates to your particular area of expertise such as sharing your triumphs, obstacles that challenged you, and strategies you implemented to overcome the challenges you faced. Share your progress and your journey. This is another way to connect to your audience. As I said previously, be who you say that you are. Show pictures of you selling your books. Have someone take pictures of you at events. Take pictures with people who purchase your books. Share reviews and photos of you in action.

You can also connect with others through the content that you create and the classes that you host, (both free classes and paid). Once you start providing information that others find valuable, information that they can take and implement into their life, or information to which they can relate, they're going to start connecting with you. Don't be surprised when you begin to receive direct messages (DMs) on your social media channels too – seize that connection and make sure you respond. When people follow you, go into their DMs and send them a small welcome message and a "Thank you." Take the opportunity to ask them questions, such as how you can help them or what they are currently struggling with. The best part about this welcoming and engagement process is that it can be automated so you don't have to manually create the messages and responses from scratch each time.

Connect with others on a real, authentic level, and you will be rewarded with real engagement and a strong brand connection.

I once "followed" a lady on Instagram that I wanted to connect with. About six hours after I sent her a friend request, she sent me a "thank you for following" message. With it, she included some pretty pictures with quotes on them. My new virtual friend added, "Hey, you can use this for a screensaver or as a cover photo on your laptop or even on your Apple watch." I was excited and felt all the warm fuzzies. I mean, who doesn't like free stuff? I thought that was such a cool touch! I decided I wanted my people to feel that same level of gratitude and thoughtfulness when they come and friend me on social media, so I went into Canva and created a screensaver, cell phone backdrop, and a smaller image that could be used as a digital watch cover. Even if people never used it, I knew the gesture would make them feel touched. A tiny bit of effort goes a long way. All it took was 10 minutes for me to create it in Canva, but the positive impact was long lasting!

Can you think of some creative ways to connect with people who may reach out to you? I encourage you to think outside the box and make your followers feel the love. What can you give for free that won't cost you anything to make? Be sure to visit www.myppbook.com to download a free checklist of ideas that you can incorporate to welcome your new followers.

#3. *Share Your Journey*

People love to feel as if they are a part of your experience. They want to be a part of your journey and share that progress with you. This is why people watch reality shows because they have an opportunity to look at other people's experiences. Then, these same viewers go and follow these people on social media, participate in dialogue and discourse, and attend virtual watch parties and discuss the episode events *because they are a part of the journey.* You can create this same momentum with your brand, but you have to be visible, and you have to be willing to share and be transparent.

We now have the 'stories' function on Instagram,

Facebook, LinkedIn, and Twitter. When I launched my first book, I was just taking pictures of what I was doing and posting them in ordinary Facebook posts. Facebook was my platform of choice back then because Instagram was still fairly new, and I wasn't comfortable with it yet, so I focused on Facebook before I started monetizing Instagram and growing my brand there. However, even without nifty features like stories back then, one of the things that helped my engagement swell in those early days was that I consistently shared my journey. Even now, if I do something as simple as take a picture of my Apple watch mileage when I exercise in the morning, that kind of post gets so much engagement because people love journeys and having insight into you as a person.

As you are in the middle of the process of writing, editing, publishing, and releasing your book, you have plenty of opportunity to *share your journey* with your followers. When you go to conferences, take pictures of what's going on. Take photos with the people who you meet and tag them when you post. When people purchase your book, shout them out on social media. Take a picture with them or ask them for a photo of them holding your book. Even if you get 10 people to purchase your book in one day, you don't have to make 10 posts that day. Post one picture every day, and you'll have content for weeks. This also has the added bonus of making it seem like you're selling books consistently. Make sure you add that hack to your toolbox; it's one of my favorites!

Last but not least, share reviews and wins. What wins

have you had lately? What kind of reviews, emails or messages have people left about your book? Have people DM'd you? If so, get their permission to screenshot their reviews, share the review and tag them online. Have people emailed you? Again, ask their permission to use them as social proof on your channels. Another way to do this more quickly is simply to blackout the person's name and just share the message that he or she sent you. Share those on your blog, on your weekly email blast, your social media, and on your website because these excerpts count as testimonials and will build your credibility over time.

The Importance of Being Consistent

If you want people to take you seriously, then you want to build an engaged audience. To do this, you must be consistent and show up on a regular basis. Disappearing for three weeks and then coming back or telling the whole entire world that you're taking a break from social media and then returning two months later breaks consistency and disrupts trust with your audience. It doesn't mean you actually have to be on social media year-round. You can take a break and use automation tools such as Planoly, Later, or Hootsuite, or Buffer to automate your posts while you are away. Nobody will ever know you're gone, but you'll still be building your brand in the process. You can still have a presence without being actively present.

An inconsistent brand is a brand that will not last long. Consistency is the key to the breakthrough. If you want to know the secret of brands that are successful, it's consistency. They show up every day, no matter how they personally feel. How can you be consistent in your business and still keep up with your current life and other responsibilities? You may be single without children or married with children. You may have a very, very packed schedule. Regardless of what your personal responsibilities are, when you start a business, you have a responsibility to your business as well, so you must be committed to consistency if you truly want success in your business.

Videos, social media stories, and reels (new) have extremely high visibility and engagement in comparison to regular posts. Unfortunately, stories posted in the stories feature deletes after 24 hours, so you need to make sure that you are posting on your stories every day to show your audience how accessible, engaging, and relatable you are. Posting six or more stories a day is plenty.

Social media is a crowded place, so the best way to stay at the top of your audience's mind is to release small bits of valuable content on a daily basis. I personally post three times a day: in the morning, the afternoon, and then in the evening. I always post a quote, a picture, and a video to attract audience members of various learning styles and to keep my content varied. If this sounds overwhelming to you, remember that you also can batch create content ahead of time. Batch-creating content means that you dedicate a block of time to creating content for several days/weeks. Then, you can use an auto scheduler to auto-post on your behalf. This option is great if you have a busy life and schedule. However, you must still be sure to engage with your audience by responding to their comments, emails, and DMs regularly.

To create more efficiency in your content production and help relieve the creative load of thinking up new ideas all the time, it's best to create a content calendar that organizes your posting schedule in advance. The most effective way to plan out your content is on a quarterly basis. Your quarterly content plan should align with your quarterly business promotions and revenue goals. Once you plan your content out for three months, you can break it down by creating a monthly focus, and then a weekly focus.

If you're new to this, an easy way to begin is to create 12 value-packed posts. One month has four weeks, so if you create one weekly post, you'll have three months' worth of posts straight away! This is an excellent place to begin if you are new or unfamiliar with social media. If you'd like to post more frequently, you can post once per day. Make sure that your posts include a short story to connect to and relate to your audience, and that your captions provide at least three action steps and offer tangible advice and relatable content. The simplest way to frame this is to identify some of the problems your targeted readers have and then position your book as the solution to their problems. Visit www.myppbook.com to access the social media planning template.

Brand Design

Remaining visible, creating targeted and engaging messaging, and connecting with your audience still trumps any color palette or font type. However, once you have these relationship building elements in place, you're going to want to make sure your brand looks attractive to your audience.

If you take a look at some of your favorite personal brands, what is it that attracts you to them? Potential clients look at you and analyze your brand in the same way that you assess other brands that interest you. Consciously cultivate a strategic eye and approach your image with meaning, because you want to be certain that your image is authentic.

One method that I implemented in the beginning stages of building my business is that I studied the branding and design of different companies. I looked at the branding of Tide, Gain, law offices, fast food restaurants, retail stores such as Walmart, and more. I studied the fonts and I assessed the impression that's created by those fonts. I thought about how the logos made me feel when I saw their name, colors, or letterhead. Some logos gave me the feeling that the company would be extremely professional, whereas others made me feel as if the company was low price and affordable for everyone.

I began to assess whether or not I could tell from the logo alone that the business was exclusive and luxurious. Consider these things as you choose the fonts that you want to use to represent your business. Make sure that you choose at least two complimentary fonts that speak to the essence of your business, mission, and how you want your brand to be perceived by others. When you've decided on two fonts, make sure that you create a spreadsheet or store them in a Google Doc, so you can give this information to your graphic designer further down the road.

When it comes to colors, it's important to be aware that colors have specific meanings as well as therapeutic qualities. Take time to research the meanings of colors as well as the effect that you want your visuals to have on potential customers when they interact with your content. For instance, many fast food restaurants use yellows, reds, and sometimes a touch of blue in their branding. This is because these colors scientifically have a stimulating effect on your appetite. Blues and greens tend to be more calming. When you go into a spa, you may see whites, grays and greens – similar colors to plants and nature because they are very serene. Each color evokes a different feeling for potential clients, so be sure you select colors that represent the mission, vision, and meaning of your brand and company goals. You also should ensure that you are aware of the psychological effects that will occur when someone looks at your brand content.

Hiring a graphic designer or learning how to use design tools is an essential step in creating professional graphics for use across your brand. You can hire a reasonably priced graphic designer on Fiverr, Upwork.com, 99 Designs, or if you find a designer that meets your budget and with whom you can build a great relationship, you can hire your design services out. If you're not yet able to pay someone, you can use free graphic design tools such as Canva so your promotional items will be attractive and still have a professional look. You can also visit creativemarket.com to purchase templates and license professional fonts. You can upload your newly purchased and downloaded fonts into Canva and create your own professional-looking graphic designs. On top of that, Canva has an entire library of tutorials in which they teach you, step-by-step, how to use the platform. If you're willing to put a little time in, it's extremely easy to learn, I promise! Remember, the goal is to present yourself as a professional consistently in your posts and with your graphics. You can create great graphics for your brand without breaking the bank.

MESSAGING

A lot of self-published authors tend to have difficulty when it comes to figuring out what their message is and learning how to align their content and their marketing with their core message. If this is an area in which you are struggling and you find you're constantly trying to gain clarity on your message, then this chapter should help you to narrow down your focus once and for all.

The first question I'm going to ask is: Who are you? When I ask this question, I'm not limiting that to your roles and responsibilities. I'm asking you, "Who are you in your authentic self? Who is it that you are without apology and without considering other people's opinions? What are your values? For what do you stand?

These are the types of elements that you should discuss and display in the content that you share and in your messaging. In order to know what makes you unique, you need to have clarity on who you are, and you must be very clear on the experiences that you've had that qualify you as a subject matter expert. After all, you've written an entire book that helps to position you as an authority in your field!

What are the concrete and specific experiences that you've had that qualify you to talk on the subject that you're addressing? Contrary to popular opinion, you don't need to have a college degree, but you *do* need to have experience, and you should be able to give solid strategies and advice. As I've said before, whatever it is you say you do, we should be able to see you doing that because success leaves clues.

If I'm asking myself these questions, my response would look like this:

> *I help authors write their books and use their book to build a high end speaking and coaching business. I do this in four ways: through teaching aspiring authors how to write, self publish, and market their book, using their books to create a signature speech, high ticket coaching and consulting programs, and teaching them how to create messaging that attracts high end clients.*

This is called a brand statement. You should be able to easily articulate exactly what it is you do, and we should see evidence of this in your marketing and branding. Visit www.myppbook.com to download a resource to help you create a brand statement of your own.

You also should keep a running record of places you speak, trainings that you host, live streams that you provide, and presentations that you create. Compile this information in one place such as a Google Doc or Excel Spreadsheet . This will help you keep your intellectual property (IP) organized and documented. Keep a running record of your intellectual property. This will allow you to understand the type of content your audience responds to and prompts them to take an extra step such as book a call, join your email list, or enroll in your programs.

You also want to use your messaging to position yourself as the go-to authority in your field. The way that you do this is by delivering content that provides value, and creating titles that speak to your audience. Share strategies to help people move the needle forward in their lives or in their businesses as it relates to your particular area of expertise. To do this, you must make the shift away from using social media just to pass the time away. Instead, use social media as business media. Instead of going through social media and liking people's random posts and reposting other people's content, videos, pictures, and quotes, make the shift to posting your own content, engaging meaningfully with your audience, sharing valuable information, strategies, and tips, and from time to time, sharing your personality and life to help your readers relate to you.

For example, share a picture of you doing something that you enjoy. Share a picture of you with your family just to let people know, *Hey, yes, I am a real person!* Personally, I talk a lot about books and provide business growth strategies on my social media pages. However, when I share pictures of me with my children or pictures of my husband and me out on a date night, people can relate to that, and they love to see those personal sides of me. Find your balance and share your human side in a way that connects with your message.

LAUNCHING YOUR BOOK

You must market and promote your book properly if you want to launch successfully. Give yourself a minimum of 30-90 days to market and promote your book before it's officially released. Don't start your marketing efforts the day of your book release. Plant seeds and prepare your potential readers for your book release well ahead of time. This can be done very, very easily by promoting and sharing content from your book on your social media channels.

One way to easily promote your book is to use theme days to plan and manage your content. Here are theme day ideas you can use to create relatable, engaging content:

- Marketing Monday- Share marketing strategies you have implemented that work.

- Talk About It Tuesday- Share tips/discuss critical or controversial issues as it relates to your topic.
- Writing Journey Wednesday- Share a behind the scenes view of your writing journey,
- Throwback Thursday- Remember who you were before all of your progress? Share a throwback picture and tell the story/lessons learned behind it.
- FAQ Friday- Answer frequently asked questions or address questions that people have but are too scared to ask.

By incorporating theme days into your marketing strategy, you will be able to create engaging and valuable content daily that connects your book and your message to your customers. Although your book may not be out yet, you'll be able to create a habit of regularly sharing content along the way, staying at the forefront of people's minds and reminding them that you have a book coming out.

Pre-Sales

Thirty days before you receive the physical copies of your book, you will need to start pre-selling your book. Pre-sales are an excellent way to make money up-front prior to your book release. This will help you generate cash flow and use the money that you make from pre-sales to offset and cover the cost of printing your books!

When I pre-sold my first book, I didn't know anything

about landing pages or book sales pages. I generated pre-sales using a simple PayPal link.

To do this, I signed up for a PayPal business account, generated the sales link, and I attached that PayPal purchase URL to the end of a social media caption where I informed my audience that my book was available for pre-order. My website wasn't even finished! I call this a minimum viable launch. A minimum viable launch is where you launch without everything being perfect- the goal is to get your product out there.

My initial launch wasn't pretty and wasn't high-end branded; however, launching imperfectly allowed me to generate thousands of dollars before my book was printed, and the pre-sales paid for the cost of my books AND my launch party! I marketed for months, shared my journey, and launched with a detailed caption, book cover, and a PayPal link.

If your website is already done or close to complete, then make sure that you create a landing page which contains an image of your book cover, the synopsis, some reviews (if you have them), and a purchase button. Then, you can send purchasers to your professionally done book sales page to read more about your book and to complete their purchase.

If you don't have a landing page ready to go, you will need to have a purchase link at the very least, so people can pay you and place an order for your book. The easiest way to do this is by creating a link through PayPal (business account), but there are other options. You can also use e-commerce tools such as Shopify, Gumroad or SamCart which both allow you to sell digital and physical products.

PayPal Pros: Widely used. Card readers and PayPal debit cards are available. Easy to print shipping labels. Instant payout available.

PayPal Cons: Can be challenging to set up. PayPal will hold your funds or take a while to set up your account if your account is new.

GumRoad Pros: Can take different payment methods. Sells physical and digital products.

GumRoad Cons: Weekly payout.

Square Pros: Card readers available.

Square Cons: Can be challenging to set up.

As I mentioned previously, you will need to give yourself a solid 30 to 90 days to promote your book, and you also should decide the platforms on which you're going to market and promote your work. You can select between Instagram and Facebook organic marketing, paid ads, or influencer marketing.

When you find influencers who resonate with your message, send them a copy of your book along with a personalized note. Make sure that your gift is nicely packaged. They may shout you and your book out on their social media channels, which has the potential of generating traffic to you, your page, and your site. Keep in mind that some influencers will not promote your work for free and may charge you a fee in exchange for promoting your book.

Here are additional marketing strategies you can use to launch your book, create anticipation, and build momentum:

- Run a contest to get reviews ahead of time.
- Select advanced readers to purchase early copies, read the book, and provide feedback and early reviews.
- Determine your actual launch day—the day you're going to mail out copies of your book and see it in bookstores. Mark this date on your calendar.
- Create an author sales page on your website.
- Start blogging and sharing your journey.
- Begin building your email list.
- Create your pitch deck and pitch the media.
- Book yourself to speak on podcasts and create a virtual book tour.
- Focus on one social media platform on which to brand yourself.
- Create videos about topics and themes in your book.
- Get booked to speak and begin sharing your message.

As well as keeping your social media active, you'll also want to plan and host a launch party. A launch party is an important opportunity for you to celebrate your hard work, and it allows your friends and family to join you in celebrating the release of your book and your new status as an author. We'll discuss launch party strategies a little later.

How To Get Reviews

As soon as possible, you'll want to start generating reviews for your book because this kind of social proof is important and helps to build your credibility. Positive reviews show healthy sales and help influence the purchasing decision of potential readers. More often than not, potential buyers usually will read reviews of your book to determine whether or not your book is worth their time.

Here are several ways to obtain book reviews:

#1. *Amazon Reviews*

You can encourage people to write Amazon reviews by including a reminder page in the back of the book that tells them, "Hey, please go onto Amazon and leave a kind review." You can give away free copies to beta readers in exchange for a review. You can give away copies of your book to people in your city, your town, your church, and people you admire. Give them a copy in exchange for leaving a review on different websites.

#2. *Host a Gift Card Giveaway*

This option allows you to give a bonus incentive to your audience for leaving you a formal review. Have your purchasers send a screenshot of their Amazon review for your book and enter them into a contest to win a gift card." Reviewers will send you screenshots to prove that they actually gave you the review. Then, you do a random draw and send a gift card to the lucky winner!

#3. *Reuse Your Reviews from Other Platforms*

Sometimes, people may post reviews for you on Facebook and LinkedIn. Remember that you can still screenshot these reviews and paste them inside of a

Google Doc, so you'll have them stored in one location. Then, you can take these same Facebook or LinkedIn reviews and put them onto your website or on your social media channels.

#4. *Publicize Your Book At Events*

Last but not least, you should get into the habit of hosting or speaking at relevant events for your niche because these are great ways to promote your book and business. If you are organizing or attending an event, make sure that you have an assistant who can work the table. After you speak, audience members are going to want to talk to you, and you can't talk and sell at the same time. You will need someone to manage the sales work while you engage with the audience, talk to them, and answer questions.

#5. *Free Gifts*

When collecting your audience's contact details, I personally found that text message marketing is a great way to collect people's emails and phone numbers in exchange for a free item. Once they go to a particular link or type in a particular number to a certain name, (For example, typing in 81010 with the keyword "author"), then that should trigger an automated response where they have to click a link, enter their name and email address, then gain access to a free training (or whatever your incentive is). Once they get the free gift, you now have a way to communicate with them and keep in contact with your most engaged audience members after your speaking engagement has ended. You can create a text message sequence that prompts questions and generates feedback about your presentation and book. Again, you can screenshot this content and keep it organized in a file for future use and reference.

Shipping

After people purchase your books from your website, you are responsible for shipping the books to everyone who ordered. This is a great opportunity to add extra details that will make you stand out.

Consider the following:

- Your shipping and packaging material
- Where you will purchase shipping and mailing supplies
- Extra goodies you will include (flyers, bookmarks, stickers, confetti)
- Whether or not you will autograph books
- Your shipping schedule
- Your method of shipping

Your Launch Party

Prior to planning your book launch, you will need to decide on your budget, your location, and the features or the layout of your party. It's important to decide on these things in advance so that you keep the party realistic and within your means. My husband and I made the grave mistake of not setting a budget for the launch of my first book, and as a result, we overspent. We had a great time, but at the end of the day, I wished that we hadn't spent as much money as we did for that one occasion. Make sure that you set a budget ahead of time, and then be sure to stay within your budget.

When I planned my launch party, we set up an RSVP list on Eventbrite where people could go online and register. People RSVP'd through the link, and once they completed registration, they received access to the location of the party.

When deciding on the location, consider access to the venue and ensure it's as easy as possible for guests to attend by car or public transportation. Consider parking fees and parking space, and inform your guests of this information well ahead of time.

It's also worth considering how many people you expect to attend. It's good to remember that when people RSVP to free events, a good rule of thumb is to expect at half the amount of people who RSVP to actually attend the event. Be prepared for more, but it will be half the number of attendees at the very least! We had 175 people who RSVP'd and 80 who attended.

Here are some additional questions you should consider when planning your launch party:

- How will your party be set up?
- Will you have someone to check everyone in?
- How will you check the list of people who attend the party against the list of people who RSVP'd?

- What is the agenda and run of show for your launch event?
- How will the party begin?
- How will you bring the party to a close?
- Will you hire DJs, photographers, or videographers?
- Are you going to need an event planner, or will you plan the event yourself?
- Will you provide food or light refreshments?

If your launch party is a live, in person event, be sure that you have an attractive signing table presentation that aligns with your overall design and includes your branding fonts and colors. You may want to put candles, pictures, or anything that will appeal to your potential readers. You should also invest in a retractable banner and branded table cover to advertise who you are, what you do, and what are the products and services that you have available.

Finally, you must make sure that you have *more than enough* books to sell. The goal is for everyone who comes to your launch event to network, connect with you, and purchase one (or several) books. That means you have to ensure you have enough books to sell as well as good pens on hand to sign books for your new readers. There's nothing more frustrating than trying to run a pen back and forth because the ink is blocked, and it won't write. I personally like Paper Mate felt tip markers because they write very smoothly, and I never have to worry about the ink not coming out. Plus, they're under $5!

Further Reading

If you're looking for further inspiration, I have a few books that would be great for you to check out. Two of these are *The One Hour Content Plan* by Meera Kothand and *The 1-Page Marketing Plan* by Allan Dib. I read both of these books at the beginning of my author journey. I knew absolutely nothing about marketing at the time, and these two books really helped me to define my brand and build a strong foundation. You also should check out *Miracle Morning Millionaires* by Hal Elrod to help you with your goal setting and time management skills. Finally, if you desire to speak, check out *Speak to Win* by Brian Tracy. It is a very good, easy-to-follow and easy-to-read book on public speaking.

Chapter 10

Your Next Steps

The goal I'm setting for you now is for you to finish your book within the next 12 to 21 days. This can be done easily and without you feeling overwhelmed because you now know how to create a strategic plan to write, self publish, and launch your book, while remaining consistent throughout the process. I wrote my first book in only two weeks, and I have helped over 1,000 others do it as well. I know you can do it, too.

Remember, you're going to make a short-term sacrifice so you can obtain long-term gains. There are so many people who want to write a book and who begin the process enthusiastically. . However, they never get around to finishing it because, at some point along the way, they throw in the towel and give up.

That's not going to be you, though, because you understand that you're going to make this short-term sacrifice, write your book on a consistent basis, and actually finish it.

You might be wondering, *How are you going to finish your book in the next 12 to 21 days?*

Well, it's quite simple.

You're going to write **one chapter per day for a set amount of days.** This is going to take focus, commitment, and dedication. Remind yourself that it's a short-term sacrifice for long-term gain.

Think about it this way: if your book has seven chapters, that means you will write one chapter per day for the next seven days. If your book has 10 or 12 chapters, then you're going to write every day for the next 10 or 12 days.

The same time that you've invested or set aside up until this point, whether it's been 15 or 30 minutes a day to do your research and activities, now is going to be spent writing—every single day. It's time for you to make the commitment.

Remember, writing your book CANNOT be something that you're going to do at the end of the day after you've finished everything else. If you want to finish your book and have been saying, "I want to write a book, but I've been struggling to finish it," this is how you finish it. You make it a priority.

Schedule the time to write one chapter per day for a set amount of days, and set aside one to two hours per day to write.

Schedule and block this time in your Google Calendar or planner. You can take one hour in the morning and one hour in the afternoon. You can take 30 minutes in the morning, 30 minutes during lunch, and one hour in the evening. The choice is yours!

Now that you have mapped out the lessons you're going to teach in each chapter, you may even find that your writing doesn't absorb all the time you set aside to write. You've already identified which of your personal stories you are going to reference in each chapter, so now it's just time to bring it all together.

Congratulations! You finally have the tools to write, self publish, and launch your book in the next 90 days, and I want to see you get it done! Let's get to it!

Authorpreneur Interview

Name: Michael Barham
Business Name: Push Elevation LLC
Website URL: www.michaelbarhamelevates.com
Facebook: http://www.facebook.com/michaelbarhamelevates
Instagram: http://www.instagram.com/michaelbarham_elevates
Twitter: http://www.twitter.com/MElevates
TikTok: http://www.tiktok.com/michaelbarhamelevates

Tell us about your book: My book *When The Ball Goes Flat* is a tangible guide to support athletes during their transition after sports.

Who is your book for and why do they need it? My book is for athletes who are having a hard time finding identity and purpose after sports end. Many athletes struggle in life after sports end because they don't have any clue on what to do next with their lives. My book helps athletes transition with confidence instead of the tradition brokenness they experience when sports is over.

What did you learn about yourself during your writing and publishing process?

I learned that I need to operate outside of my comfort zone more. The process showed me that I could execute at a higher level if I planned ahead of time. The process instilled a high level of confidence in me and made me realize how much harvest is available if you commit to doing whatever it takes.

What advice would you offer to professionals who desire to write a book?

The first thing I would advise someone looking to write a book would be to get a coach. I've wanted to write my own book for 5 years and I was stuck. I connected with Jasmine and the team and got my first draft completed in 3 days!

The second thing I advise is for them not to wait for the perfect time because it will never come. I got my book done at the most inconvenient time in my life. I left thousands of dollars on the table previously waiting for the perfect time.

You need a book right now if you are looking to become an authority figure in your lane. Writing my book has gotten me media interviews which has increased my authority. I've instantly gained a different level of respect from authority figures in my industry that I've known for 5 or more years.

Epilogue

Now that you have reached the end of this book, you have the information and strategies to write and publish your book successfully. You have the opportunity to package your story in a way that creates opportunities, increases your influence, and leaves a legacy for generations to come.

Don't just read this book and sit it on the shelf. Put it into action. Implement the strategies. Write your book and impact the world.

The following is a summary of the concepts that have been discussed in this book to help you become a successful author:

Chapter 1: The Mindset of a Best-Selling Author: This chapter helps you understand the mindset you must have to go from being an author who just wants to tell his or her story to an author who creates an impactful book that changes the world.

Chapter 2: Embrace Your Voice: Learn how to share your story authentically while protecting your most personal information. Understand your rights and protect your work from theft.

Chapter 3: Niche Your Topic: Gain clarity about your topic, understand the value you provide, and learn how to align your story and book with audiences and organizations that will benefit from what you provide.

Chapter 4: Research and Relevance: Write a book that people want and need instead of the book you want to write. Learn how to use various social media websites to conduct research on your ideal reader, so you can create premium content for your book.

Chapter 5: Writing Your Book: Understand the five phases of the writing process and learn how to create an accountable writing plan, so you can write and publish your book in a matter of weeks successfully.

Chapter 6: Creating Your Money Title: Learn how to write a book title that engages your target audience and repels potential readers who will not turn into clients.

Chapter 7: Designing Your Book Cover: Understand the required components to design an eye-catching book cover.

Chapter 8: The Revision Process: Learn all about the editing process and identify how to protect yourself and your work in the process.

Chapter 9: Promoting Your Book: Get ideas to sell your book and make your launch a success!

Chapter 10: Your Next Steps: It's time for you to bring all the strategies you've learned together and put your plan into action.

There's no more time to procrastinate. It's time for you to believe in yourself, implement these strategies, write your book, and impact the world for ages to come. Someone's breakthrough is depending on your book.

About the Author

Jasmine Womack is a writing consultant for career professionals, coaches, speakers, and consultants. She also speaks and provides training in the areas of personal development, diversity, equity, and inclusion.

Jasmine is a graduate of Redan High School in Stone Mountain, GA. She then attended Fort Valley State University, where she graduated with a B.S. in Middle Grades Education. Afterwards, she served as a middle school language arts teacher in the DeKalb County School District. During this time, she obtained an M.Ed. in Curriculum and Instruction, as well as an Ed.S. in Educational Leadership from Columbus State University. Jasmine went on to teach for two years in the Cobb County School District. During her tenure as an educator, she also served as the school's writing coach, team lead, department chair, and model classroom teacher.

After 10 years in the classroom, Jasmine wrote her first book, *Twenty Pearls of Wisdom: A Woman's Guide to Self-Preservation*. Her publication journey was filled with difficult lessons and set Jasmine on the path of author entrepreneurship. From her experiences self-publishing a book through an online vanity publisher, Jasmine knew she wanted to help other aspiring authors accomplish their dream of writing and publishing a book and help them avoid many of the pitfalls she experienced. She desired to help them avoid the situations she encountered that cost her time, mental peace, and money.

Following the release of her first book, Jasmine decided to create an online virtual challenge based on the principles in her book. After promoting her challenge on Facebook, to her surprise, over 400 people signed up in fewer than 10 days. She later turned this into a paid challenge and started a paid membership community in which she was able to teach life principles based on her book in more detail.

This was the beginning of an avalanche of business. After the membership community came speaking engagements, opportunities to publish books for others, digital products, masterclasses, courses, and high-ticket coaching programs. All of this started from one book.

Jasmine is the founder of Author Made Easy® Bootcamp, where she teaches career professionals and service providers how to start, write, publish, and launch their books, create viral visibility, and build their coaching programs.

She is also the founder of Six Figure Storyteller™ Mastermind, a 12-month coaching program in which she helps published authors turn their books into a high-ticket group coaching program.

Jasmine has worked with over 400 authors and helped them start, grow, and expand their author-entrepreneur businesses as well as inspired over 10,000 people through her social media platforms.

Jasmine has been featured in major publications such as *Forbes*, *HuffPost*, and *Voyage ATL*.

Her goal is to help others use their stories to impact and change the world.

Hire Jasmine to Speak at Your Event

www.jasminewomack.com/speaking

Presentation Topics

The Power of Your Story: Using Your Story to Market and Grow Your Business Online

You can build trust and cohesiveness through storytelling. Storytelling allows you to connect with your clients and speak to their hearts and minds through sharing experiences to which your audience can relate. Story marketing positions you to be a better leader, provide solution-based products and services, and become the go-to professional in your field.

Attendees will learn:

1. How to use your story to make sure people see you, hear you, and understand exactly why they must engage with you and purchase your book, other products, and services.
2. The 5-Step Story Method to help you write engaging captions and content that converts readers and scrollers into pay-in-full clients.
3. How to transform client stories into strong testimonials that build trust, credibility, and attract clients who are eager to pay you in full.

Published and Paid: How to Write, Publish, and Market a High-Quality Book in 12 Weeks or Less

As a corporate professional or small business owner, writing a book is not an option. Establish your legacy, create more fulfillment and purpose in your life, and attract high-end clients in your business.

Attendees will learn:

1. The simple method to share your story effectively in a way that engages readers (even if you don't know where to start or have struggled for years).
2. 5 keys to write a high-quality book quickly that will get you booked speaking engagements and high-end clients.
3. How to leverage technology and local resources to make your writing and self publishing experience a breeze.
4. How to utilize the power of social media to grow your audience, create your digital footprint, and establish yourself as an authority in your industry.
5. The three formats in which your book needs to be published to obtain maximum reach and revenue.

Bankable Books: How to Use Your Book to Launch a Profitable Speaking and Coaching Career

95% of self published authors make less than $1,000 per year from their book. You must have a concrete plan for building a profitable business beyond the book.

Attendees will learn:

1. How to use your book to outline your signature speech in less than 10 minutes.
2. How to leverage your book launch to attract high-end coaching clients.
3. How to use your book to create the curriculum for your coaching program.
4. What a book funnel is and why you should have one.
5. Automation systems and tools to have in place, so you can convert readers into clients with ease.

Execution Over Excuses: Take Your Ideas from Concept to Creation by Using Systems and Automation to Harmonize Your Life and Business

Take your idea from your head to paper to action by using strategies and systems to create a business without overwhelming yourself. This presentation is ideal for mompreneurs or those with a busy life who want to operate a successful business.

In this session, *attendees will learn*:

- How to create a morning routine to position yourself for success.
- How to align your ideas with your big picture goals and life and business plan.
- How to use measurable, realistic, attainable, and timely benchmarks to develop and plan your goals.
- The 5 Step MEDIA method to strategically use social media to grow your brand and get clients
- Business systems to develop and automate your workflow

Work With Jasmine

Access Free Resources and Your Digital Toolkits:
www.publishedandpaidbook.com

Digital Products and Self-Study Options:
www.jasminewomack.com/store

Bankable Books 5-Part Video Series: Learn the Secret Behind Writing a Book that Brings you $8k-$10k per month or more
Visit www.jasminewomack.com

www.sixfigurestorytellerlive.com

ONE WEEKEND CAN CHANGE YOUR LIFE. JOIN ME FOR THIS ONCE IN A LIFETIME EXPERIENCE!

Six Figure Storyteller Live: A 3-Day Conference for Aspiring and Published Non-Fiction Authors Who Are Ready to Leverage Their Story and Have Their Expertise Start Working for Them.

Learn more about the Six Figure Storyteller Live experience at www.sixfigurestorytellerlive.com